VIETNAM
BEFORE - DURING - AFTER

A YOUNG MAN'S JOURNEY

David C. Friend

TRILOGY CHRISTIAN PUBLISHERS
TUSTIN, CALIFORNIA

Trilogy Christian Publishers
A Wholly Owned Subsidary of Trinity Broadcasting Network
2442 Michelle Drive Tustin, CA 92780

First Trilogy Christian Publishing hardcover edition September 2018

Trilogy Christian Publishing/ TBN and colophon are trademarks of Trinity Broadcasting Network.

For information about special discounts for bulk purchases, please contact Trilogy Christian Publishing.

Manufactured in the United States of America

10 9 8 7 6 5 4 3 2 1

Library of Congress Cataloging-in-Publication Data is available.

ISBN: 978-1-64088-135-8

ISBN: 978-1-64088-136-5 (eBook)

My friend David Friend has been a pastor for over 20 years, and has served the people he has been entrusted with faithfully. His book Vietnam Before-During-After: A young man's journey is a powerful and vulnerable story that illustrates how God can turn anything around for His glory. This book will inspire you and encourage you to pursue God no matter what circumstances come your way.

John Bevere
Author/Speaker
Messenger International

DAVID C. FRIEND

• DEDICATION •

Dedicated to my wife Sharon.
Thank you for your encouragement.

DAVID C. FRIEND

VIETNAM

When I left the Republic of Vietnam, I never wanted to talk about anything I experienced there again. The worst day of my life was March 20, 1967. It was the day I landed at the Bien Hoa air base in Vietnam. For many years, I believed the best day of my life was March 18, 1968, the day I left Vietnam and landed at Travis Air Force Base in northern California.

For many years my wife and I almost never discussed my experiences in Vietnam. However, over the past few years something has been stirring in my heart. What happened to the men with whom I served?

What are the challenges these 18 to 20 year-old men have experienced and are facing today? If it was not for my wife encouraging me to write about my time there, I probably would have never written this book.

As a pastor for over 20 years, I have met and given counsel to many of the men who served in that small country nearly 9,000 miles from America. Many of these men have learned to hide their physical and emotional wounds. Thankfully, many of these veterans are active in the Veterans of Foreign Wars or other veterans programs. They have found help through these organizations.

The Vietnam veteran was young compared to other wars. They returned to an America divided about whether we should have been there. Because of my service in Vietnam my heart is deeply touched for those who served there. My prayers are for their families who waited and prayed for them to come home. Tragically, over 58,200 made the ultimate sacrifice.

In some small way, may my life experiences before, during, and after Vietnam help you understand what young Americans faced during one of our country's most turbulent times.

The challenges I faced in Vietnam are not mentioned in order to make you feel sorry for me. Many soldiers faced far more difficult conditions than I experienced. All I can offer to you are my personal encounters. As you read through these pages, try to imagine what approximately 2,700,000 men and women would have faced before, during, and after Vietnam.

What did those serving in Vietnam think about the protests and riots happening in America? How did they feel about being called "baby killers, rapists, and murderers" after they came home? Vietnam has been called an unpopular war. Our country was torn apart trying to deal with this war. The actions we took in Vietnam were dictated by the political interests of many in Washington, DC. Decisions were being made by powerful men with evil intentions.

For decades, Vietnam veterans have kept silent about their service. Only in recent years has America shown their appreciation to the Vietnam soldier.

Thankfully, Americans are welcoming home those who have fought in Desert Storm, Afghanistan, and Iraq. Today our prayers go out to the men and women who have volunteered to serve in our military. I am proud to say the men and women in our Armed Forces today are as fine as any of those who have ever served our country.

Although I was not a Christian, I believe the Lord helped me through times of loneliness, fear, and despair. May this story reveal God's faithfulness to those who seek Him. My desire is that you will be better prepared to face the challenges in your life after seeing how so many veterans have withstood theirs.

This is an attempt to show the life of one 20-year-old man before, during, and after Vietnam.

Table of Contents

SECTION I - Before Vietnam

Chapter 1. Life Was Good..1

Chapter 2. Wake Up Call.. 13

Chapter 3. Do Everything They Say..23

Chapter 4. On My Way 37

SECTION II - During Vietnam

Chapter 5. Entering the Country..49

Chapter 6. Formation Call 61

Chapter 7. Assignments 71

Chapter 8. Relationships in Vietnam..................................87

Chapter 9. Expect the Unexpected.....................................99

Chapter 10. Tet Offensive 113

Chapter 11. Short Timer 131

SECTION III - After Vietnam

Chapter 12. Coming Home 141

Chapter 13. Friends of Vietnam... 155

Chapter 14. Blessed in Vietnam.. 163

Chapter 15. Influence 173

Chapter 16. Bone Marrow Cancer 181

Chapter 17. The Wall.. 191

Chapter 18. After the War 199

Chapter 19. Looking Back - My Opinion 207

Not life but good life is to be chiefly valued.

SOCRATES

SECTION I

Before Vietnam

Life Was Good

When I look back at my life in the late 1950's and 1960's, it was pretty good. As a matter of fact, it was amazing. These were my high school and college years. We were what I call the "Disneyland generation." The Mickey Mouse Club was in full swing. My number one vacation request was a trip to Disneyland. That is until I hit the ripe old age of 16. Most of my friends in school felt like I did. As we entered the decade of the 60's, rock and roll music became our primary focus. Overall, life was good.

For most of us high school had many memories, both good and bad. There were a lot of activities in school in which we could participate. However, joining the 4-H club, key club, or ROTC was not for me.

Little did we know our government was up to no good by becoming involved in the tiny country of Vietnam. Our President and politicians were entering a no-win situation. Sadly, many of our politicians knew it was an impossible undertaking. At first, the American people had faith in their leaders. They were confident we would never get into anything that was not justifiable. But a major war in Vietnam was on the horizon. It would negatively impact the lives of millions of Americans. This war divided America.

Vietnam was not even on my radar screen. It was the early 60's and my thoughts were on working in order to buy my first car. It was a 1953 Chevy Bel Air, a four-door rusted out car from Ohio. My dad said it was the perfect car for me. I don't know how perfect it was, but it fit my budget of $150. I was so proud to pay cash. After patching all the rust, I paid $29.95 for a new Earl Scheib paint job. Why I decided to paint it lime green is still a mystery to me. That car was the key to finding new ways to make money and get dates with the girls at South Mountain High School.

Sometimes my fellow classmates would pay me for a ride to school. Their parents were happy to pay me and I was happy to get the extra cash. My '53 Chevy was a profit center. During my high school years we were on double session. The High School in South Phoenix had far too many students. I attended the morning session from 7 AM to 12 noon. It was great because I could get part-time jobs after school. I had jobs with several different companies at one time. Sweeping bowling lanes, stocking shelves at a candy store, delivering door-to-door flyers, cleaning the grill at a hot dog restaurant, and making frozen fruit snacks were just some of my jobs.

Having my own car opened up new opportunities for me. Soon I discovered having a car made it easier to get a date. You could say I was a little obsessed with my car. Saturday mornings were spent washing and polishing every square inch of my '53 Chevy.

However, it did not take long for me to realize a four-door family sedan was not the attraction I thought it was. Therefore, I traded it in for a 1956 Chevy two-door coupe. Now, I had arrived.

With school, work, and dating my schedule was packed. I never thought about Vietnam. Occasionally a friend would tell me they were volunteering to go into the Marines or some branch of the military so they could go to Vietnam. That was fine for them, but I wanted something different. College seemed to be a better option for me. Besides, I was the last of four kids living at home. I had the house to myself. (Of course my parents were there.)

Even though I have said life was good to me back then; I can think of a few bumps in my road. One day my sister Jan asked if she could borrow my car in order to pick up something. After much consternation I said it was okay but I told her to be very, very, very careful. So off she went with my pride and joy. About two hours later she walked into the house and said she had a little problem but had it fixed. Now, the words "little problem" and "had it fixed" did not go over very well with me. As I ran outside I discovered the right door of my beautiful two-door 1956 Chevy looked like it had an encounter with a tank. Jan had scraped the side of my car against a telephone pole. She took the car to a body shop where they tried to hammer and pull everything back into place. Well, it looked like it had been hammered. Needless to say it was the last time I loaned my car to anyone. In case you are wondering, my sister and I laugh about that incident today —at least she does.

Regretfully, in high school I did not focus on academics. Math and history were my favorites and I did well with them, but working and dating beat out everything else. As if I did not have enough going on, I decided to join a rock 'n roll band. It was called the King Bees. The guys needed a drummer so I bought a set of drums and took some lessons. Soon, we were playing at high school dances and store openings. You could say life was really good.

While all of this was going on in my life I would hear about the police action taking place in a country half a world away from me called Vietnam.

Like a typical teenager I did not read the newspaper or watch the nightly news on television. However, I started to notice more of my friends were joining the military so they could fight against the advancement of communism in Vietnam. At least that was what they were told it was about.

Ed, who was a school friend of mine from first grade through high school, joined the Marines. He was homecoming King and quarterback of the football team, and an A student. Did I mention he was dating one of the cheerleaders? With all of the great things happening in his life, Ed was the last person who I thought would give up his good life for the Marines. After all, he had the coolest car on campus— a 1957 Chevy two-door hardtop with dual exhausts and a 327 V8 engine. Ladies, you can ask any car guy about Ed's car. It was the ultimate chick magnet. You will hear more about Ed in a later chapter.

While some of my friends went into the military, I decided to go to college. The first year was great. I continued my multiple part-time jobs with an 18-hour-per-semester class load. Our rock band was doing great. Life was still good to me.

On September 25, 1965, while I was in my sophomore year at Phoenix College, I met the most amazing girl. Her name was Sharon McCray. We met at a teenage dance place called The Hungry Eye in North Phoenix. It was the place to be in 1965 in Phoenix, Arizona. I was there as a backup drummer for another rock group performing at The Hungry Eye. The drummer of the group was my friend and had called to see if I could back him up because he was feeling sick and might need me to cover for him.

Sharon was there with two of her friends. Since I was a backup for the drummer, I had a free night to meet some of the girls who were there. Looking around, I noticed three young ladies standing off to the side of the dance floor. Being the arrogant person I was, it looked like an opportunity to meet three potential dance partners. I walked up to these girls and asked the first one on the left to dance. She was cute and pleasant but I walked her back to her other two friends after one dance. There stood Sharon in the middle. So I asked her to dance and she said okay.

After that first dance I realized this was not just another girl. I asked Sharon if we could talk for a while. She was sweet, beautiful, and even laughed at my dumb jokes. We spent an hour or so just talking. During our talk I was hoping my friend Sam, who was the drummer I was there to back up for, would not get sick and need me to cover for him. Soon the other two girls Sharon came with said they needed to go. They had come together in Sharon's car. As we were ending our conversation I asked Sharon for her phone number. She was wondering if she should give it to me or give a fake number. Sharon was also wondering if my last name was really Friend and if I could be trusted.

But then I thought, *How could she not give me her number?* After all, I was a drummer in a rock band. She would not miss this opportunity. Again, I asked for her number. Hesitantly, Sharon gave me a phone number. On the way home I could not think of anything except this beautiful girl I had just met. When I got home that night I told my family that Sharon was the one. She was the best girl I had ever met. The next day I called Sharon and she answered. She had given me her real number. From that day on I stopped dating anyone else. I cut my mop-style hair and dropped out of the band. Sharon became my number one priority. We began dating every weekend. We talked for hours and hours on the phone and on our dates. She was the girl for me. Life was good.

With my life so full, I paid little attention to what was happening in the tiny country of Vietnam. However, more and more of my high school and work acquaintances were now being drafted. They were going to a war in a tiny country thousands of miles from Phoenix, Arizona. Soon I began to hear about guys I knew who were wounded or killed in Vietnam. Then I begin to wonder why America was even there.

To understand why we were in Vietnam we need to go back to the Presidency of John F. Kennedy. His advisors convinced him we needed to help the people of South Vietnam stop the spread of communism. In May 1961, Kennedy authorized the use of American military advisors in Vietnam. The advisory group rapidly grew to several thousand. Then on November 22, 1963, President Kennedy was assassinated in Dallas Texas. That afternoon, Vice President Lyndon Baines Johnson became our President.

This was the first time I showed any real interest in government and politics. Vietnam was becoming a major concern to our country and our politicians. However, it was still of little concern to me. President Johnson decided to increase our involvement in Vietnam. He did not want to be known as a weak president and decided to put the lives of hundreds of thousands of young American men and women at risk. At the time of President Kennedy's assassination, America had approximately 16,000 troops, a.k.a. "advisors," in Vietnam. By 1966, America's presence in Vietnam grew to almost 400,000. In 1967, the year I went to Vietnam, 500,000 American lives were at stake.

As the war in Vietnam grew, my love for Sharon had grown to the point where I wanted to spend the rest of my life with her. It was in September 1966 that I entered my sophomore year of college. I was studying to be a high school history teacher. My life was full of dreams, work, college, and my wife-to-be, Sharon McCray. Life was good. Church, the Bible, Christian people were not a part of my life. After all, I figured I had it all. Why did I need to go to church?

Later, I realized without the Lord I had nothing at all. If only I would've known Proverbs 16:9, *"We can make our plans but the Lord determines our steps."* (NLT)

LIFE APPLICATION

We have all experienced times in our lives when we thought "Life is good." It may have been at our high school prom or graduation, or when we started to date someone special. Then there were times when life seemed to give us a raw deal. Regardless of what we may experience in life, we can trust our God to carry us through.

You can see why I said life was good.

We started our relationship on Sep 25, 1965.

Thirteen months later the US Army would call on me.

We had fun whatever we did. Sometimes a drive around town was all we could afford to do. My brown eyed girl in my 1961 Plymouth Belvedere made life very good.

"Arise, Shine, for your Light has come."

ISAIAH 60:1 NIV

DAVID C. FRIEND

CHAPTER 2

Wake Up Call

During the 1960s America was divided in its opinions of the war in Vietnam. The 60s were considered to be one of the most tumultuous political and cultural times in the history of the United States. When 1960 came around, many called it "The Dawn of the Golden Age," — a time of prosperity and growth.

On January 20, 1961, John F. Kennedy became President of the United States of America. He was a young, handsome, hero, charismatic and wealthy. The Golden Age quickly became the age of political unrest, and the battle for civil rights. The country was torn apart with the assassination of President Kennedy and the Vietnam War. This was the most divided America had been since the Civil War.

Let's take a look at some of the significant events of 1965, 1966, and 1967 in the United States of America.

1) The number of American troops in Vietnam grew to over 500,000.

2) The Marines amphibious assault on Vietnam was the largest landing since the Korean War.

3) In Mississippi, protesters for civil rights were tear gassed.

4) The American Nazi party in Dallas tried to test the law.

5) US Army F-105 bombers start strategic target bombing in North Vietnam.

6) Thirty-thousand Americans protest down New York's Fifth Avenue to stop American activities in Vietnam.

7) World heavyweight boxing champion Cassius Clay, later known as Mohammed Ali, refuses the draft.

8) A sniper kills 14 at University of Texas.

9) The number of US troops killed in Vietnam reaches 6,358.

10) David C. Friend's student deferment taken away. He was reclassified as 1-A for the draft. (This was significant to me.)

Little did I know how my life would be radically changed by the tiny country of Vietnam. My wake- call came in the mail the first week of October 1966. The Selective Service board had decided to change my classification from 2-S "student deferment," to 1-A "eligible for immediate duty." The letter came about one month after I signed up for 14 semester hours at Phoenix College. A student deferment now required 15 semester hours. Had this happened before I registered at college, I would have increased my number of semester hours. The administration office at Phoenix College said it was too late to increase my hours.

In addition to needing more hours, students were required to have a high grade point average. Because I was a C student with an occasional A or B, my grades did not qualify me for a student deferment. President Johnson wanted more bodies in Vietnam and he would do whatever was necessary to get them.

The President and his Secretary of Defense, Robert McNamara, even recorded their arrogant conversations about getting more soldiers to Vietnam.

Now I was caught in the Vietnam build up. Confused, I called the selective service board to find out how soon I could be drafted. The representative said to expect a draft notice within a week or so. That is when I went to the recruitment office to see what options were available to me. The recruiting sergeant said if I would volunteer for the draft, I would get a better assignment. He advised me that only a two-year commitment should keep me from being sent to Vietnam. Well as you probably guessed, he did not tell me the truth, the whole truth, and nothing but the truth.

Being a naive 19-year-old guy, I took his advice and volunteered to be drafted. Within a few days, I was given the army's acceptance of my decision and told to report for my physical examination. As I recall, my physical was scheduled for October 18, 1966. When I went in for my appointment, about 50 to 75 young men were going through the same process as me. Some were drafted, some volunteered for the draft, and others had signed up for the regular Army. Between 25,000 to 30,000 men were being drafted or volunteering for the military each month. The military set a monthly quota. All they wanted was more bodies, regardless of the trauma to families.

The day I reported to the induction center was like getting into a New York subway car. We were rushed through answering dozens of questions and a physical examination. The physical exam was one of the most degrading things I had ever experienced. During this rush hour examination time I was not aware my answers were becoming the law in the Army's case to sign me up for duty. How many forms I signed and what the forms said was unclear to me. But why should I be concerned? This was the final step in the process of becoming a member of the U.S. Army. After all, I would probably get a great assignment in Europe or the states.

During one of the tests, a doctor asked if I had any physical problems. Without thinking about the importance of his question, I quickly told him I had a kidney stone about two years prior.

By this time my testosterone had kicked in. I felt I was in competition with all of these other guys to be accepted. During the examination I did not reveal all of my prior kidney issues. Kidney stones were growing in me every few months. Often I would pass a stone or two, with kidney or bladder infections.

A few months after my physical examination I was told I should have gone through further testing and may have been eligible for a medical discharge. Oh well, if that would have happened I would not have been able to write this book.

After passing the examination, we were gathered into a large room and told to raise our right hand and repeat after the officer in charge. We took our oath of enlistment.

"I, David C. Friend, do solemnly swear I will support and defend the Constitution of the United States against all enemies, foreign and domestic; I will bear true faith and allegiance to the same; and I will obey the orders of the president of the United States and the orders of the officers appointed over me, according to regulations and the Uniform Code of Military Justice, so help me God."

Little did I know how much I would need God to help me over the next two years.

Wow, I did it, I thought. *I am going to Europe. Sharon and I can get married so we can go together.* After the oath, the officer in charge told us to check the bulletin board for our date and time to be sent to basic training. Looking over the bulletin board, I discovered something that I thought must be a mistake. There it was, "David C. Friend. Report to Sky Harbor Airport at midnight, 18 October 1966." *Wait a minute,* I thought, *that was tonight.* As I walked over to the officer in charge I noticed he had a different look on his face. When I told him something must be wrong he responded with, "Soldier, you will address me as 'Sir.' You are in the Army. The Army never makes a mistake. You are ordered to report as posted or else you will be arrested. If you do not show up tonight, the military police will consider you AWOL (absent without leave) and place you in confinement until your prison sentencing." Uh oh, they were not as friendly to me as the recruiting sergeant. All of his kind words became a distant memory.

When I left the induction center, I was thinking surely they must give us a few days or a week to get our personal things settled. Well, I was wrong. I was in the Army now.

The name on the building should've told me something. After all, it did say "Induction Center," not "future-trip-planning center." My first call was to my girl Sharon. Without thinking I asked her what she was doing tonight. Then I told her what had just happened. Sharon was still at work when I called. We would get together after she got off of work. Then I called my Dad and told him the news. He said, "Let's get the family together." At midnight, Sharon and my family were at the airport. All of this was so surreal.

This was my first time on an airplane. It was a four-engine prop commercial airline. About 60 to 70 new recruits loaded onto the plane. As we taxied down the runway, I looked out the window and saw those I loved, waving as if they could see me. Most of the guys on board were leaving wives, family, and friends to face a new set of challenges. We saw the lights of Phoenix disappear. My feelings were mixed. Excitement, confusion, and fear bounced around in my mind. Hundreds of questions raced through my thoughts about my future plans. The most significant wake-up call of my life became my new reality. My plans to get married and move to someplace in Europe with Sharon looked a little questionable. All of a sudden I was concerned about my lack of a relationship with God. Would He turn His back on me? Would He answer my prayers, or ignore them?

Most of the guys on the plane had been drafted, maybe 25% were regular Army, and about 10% of us had volunteered for the draft. Basic training would be at Fort Bliss, Texas. The nearest city was El Paso. I remembered driving through El Paso as a child. Oh how I wished we would fly past El Paso and back to Phoenix, Arizona.

Soon I would be facing another wake-up call. It would be called, "Reveille."

LIFE APPLICATION

Life is filled with wake-up calls for everyone. Maybe your wake-up call was the loss of a friend or a financial failure. Regardless of the reason, a wake-up call can be an opportunity for a new beginning, a fresh start, or a time of reevaluating your purpose. I believe the Lord has a plan for your life. He created you with a purpose. Although wake-up calls may be filled with new challenges; they may be one of the best things we will face if we look for the purpose of the call.

DEC · 66

Basic training at Fort Bliss, Texas tried to take me from a Rock and Roll drummer to a disciplined soldier. I had no idea what was in my future.

FEP • 67

Advanced Individual Training was at Fort Ord, California. In the middle of my training I received my assignment to The Republic of Vietnam. My training was modified to include jungle survival and combat zone readiness.

"Mine is not to reason why."

LORD TENNYSON

Do Everything They Say

The pilot said, "Fasten your seatbelts." We started our descent into the El Paso airport. The atmosphere in the plane was so thick you could have cut it with a knife. Some of the men were trying to say something funny. One guy shouted, "When do we get to eat?" Someone else said, "Where are the women in El Paso?" Everyone was nervous. Personally, I was already missing my good life with my girl Sharon. How I wished I could live in Phoenix, go to work, and continue with school. Even going to hear a sermon at the Southern Baptist Church would be better than this. At this time, I had not yet become a Christian.

Once again I asked God to be with me. Would He help me or would He let me go it alone? Little did I know how many people were praying for me, especially those at the Southern Baptist Church. Something inside me made me feel this won't be bad. After all, I knew of several guys, including my brother, Jim, and my brother-in-law, Rich, who had survived military basic training. They came out alright.

The plane came to a stop and we were escorted to a green army bus. That is when every man who was dressed in green fatigues started yelling at us. My thoughts were, Why all the cussing and yelling orders at the new recruits? During the bus ride to Fort Bliss, a mean-looking man in a smoky bear hat walked up and down the aisle, cussing and calling us every name in the book. He said he was a drill sergeant. I thought, What is a drill sergeant?

I quickly discovered not to make eye contact with this verbally aggressive man. Looking straight ahead was our best course of action. One poor guy looked up at the drill sergeant and asked a question about where we were going and how soon we would get there. That Drill Sergeant made an example of him, saying, "I will ask the questions!" He continued, "Your job for the next eight weeks is to do everything I say and do it without questioning me." Then he bent down and looked straight into the guy's face and said, "Do you understand?" He said, "Do you understand?" several more times. The bus pulled into Fort Bliss at about three a.m. It was pitch black. As we were getting off the bus, I asked the guy next to me, "What is all of this about?" He was my age and had volunteered for the draft. He gave me the best advice anyone could have given. It was only four words, "Do everything they say." Those words went deep inside of me and became my course of action for the next eight weeks.

When I was inducted into the Army I weighed 119 pounds and was 5-foot 6-inches tall. It made me the smallest guy in my company. Little did I know in a few weeks, I would gain 24 pounds of muscle and look like a gymnast. My small, muscular frame became an advantage in most of the physical training we would face.

We did not get to bed until around 4:00 a.m. Then, before the sun came up, a loudspeaker came on with the most horrible screeching sound. Instantly, we became familiar with something they called, "Reveille," or "the first call." That bugle was driving us crazy. I wanted to scream out, "Enough is enough!" Thankfully, the advice of my new friend overruled my reaction. "Do everything they say." As we got out of bed, we were still in our civilian underwear. Soon we would march to a building filled with clothes, and this would be our new fashion statement.

The drill sergeant who was yelling at us on the bus was in our barracks. He started pulling guys out of bed, throwing pillows, sheets, and bedding all over the place. We all thought he must never sleep. Even at 5:30 AM, the man's clothing looked like it was made of cardboard. We could see our reflection in his boots. He walked as stiff as a board. Standing 6'3" and weighing a very muscular 220 pounds, he was an intimidating figure. The man put the fear of God in all of us. I already had a fear of God and did not need any more.

Our Drill Sgt. was an African-American and I felt like he was tougher on the black guys in our company than the Hispanics or whites. Somehow this man was able to get about 110 recruits lined up to go eat breakfast. Now dressed in our civilian clothes, we marched to the mess hall to eat.

There were four things challenging me at 5:30 AM. First, instead of a screeching bugle to wake us up, why not an alarm clock? Second, why did we have to march to go eat? Third, why did we have to climb a ladder and reach out hand over hand on bars 10 feet off the ground to get permission to eat? Fourth, why did they call where we were going to eat the "mess hall"?

As soon as we entered the mess hall, I understood the name. All I wanted was a bowl of Cheerios, a piece of toast, and a glass of orange juice and I would be fine. However, I was handed a metal tray with several separated sections. The tray looked like those I had seen in movies about prison life. We walked sideways, while the Drill Sgt. was cussing at us and telling us to "Move, move, move!" The guy behind the cafeteria-style counter would drop a glob of white gravy with brown lumps onto the tray. They called it "SOS." I won't interpret. Then he slapped a pile of greasy potatoes and some undercooked scrambled eggs on my prison tray. At the end of the line, I was given a mug of black coffee. They did not ask me if I liked coffee. I felt like asking if they had any cereal or telling them that I do not like coffee and that I don't like scrambled eggs uncooked. About the time I thought about saying something the words, "do everything they say," came to mind.

This is a good time to comment on the words, "do everything they say." When young recruits are being trained to defend our country and their fellow soldiers, they need to be disciplined. The key factor in our training was to have a disciplined life. To learn to take orders and do whatever they said. If it was an order it did not have to make sense to me. Just do it. (Nike used that 40 years later.)

When I was a boy growing up, my dad believed in discipline. He used a belt to spank my brother and I. My sisters received their spankings with his bare hand. The effect of those spankings helped prepare me for the discipline I had to learn in the Army.

Today many believe spanking a child is wrong. Some will come against parents who spank their children. Now, I do not believe that a spanking should ever cause injury to a child. Personally, I thank my dad for disciplining his children. He told us he never enjoyed spanking us. But the end result (pun intended) was discipline.

Today as a believer, I have read the many references to discipline we see in God's word. A passage of Scripture that I have always found to be helpful is in Hebrews 12:11 (NLT) which says, *"No discipline is enjoyable while it is happening—it's painful! But afterward there will be a peaceful harvest of right living for those who are trained in this way."* Discipline is vital in any phase of our life.

Some of you may wonder why I am going into detail about my first few days of basic training and the discipline we needed. Those who have experienced basic training in the military know what I am talking about.

America was at war with the Communists in Vietnam. We were sending 18 to 22 year-old new recruits into a war zone. The backgrounds of these young men were varied. Some came from a farm, others were from a big city. Still others had ROTC training in high school or college. Most of us had never shot a rifle or handgun. Yet, all of us needed to be prepared to face the most dangerous place on earth. We desperately needed to be trained vigorously, because our lives would depend on it.

At night, when we tried to get some sleep for the next day's arduous training, we might hear a guy crying or someone cussing about a judge who had told him it's the Army or jail. In every case we must all come through basic training as soldiers who were disciplined for service to their country.

Personally, I believe many of our high school graduates today would benefit from a few weeks of basic training. The discipline of such training would be of value to our country. This could take place before they go on to college or a career. This is not a recommendation that everyone should go into the military. However, a few weeks of physical and mental discipline would strengthen our young men and women.

As my training continued, I discovered it made my body increase in strength and stamina. Since I was the smallest guy in our company, many expected me not to be able to perform well in the physical challenges of the military.

However, in the last week of our training we had a companywide competition to test the skills we had been taught. There were five performance activities we all had to go through. Almost everyone, including me, was surprised at the results at the end of the fourth event. The soldier with the highest score was Private Friend. That was me. Now, I am not bragging, but it felt pretty good to be on top after seven weeks of being persecuted for my lack of physical size. The final test was the mile run. This was my weakest event, and I finished in the middle of the pack. Yet, due to my overall score, the final standing showed me as the number two man in the entire company of over 120. Again, please forgive me for this personal story, but I learned something great about the military that day. The men were cheering for my accomplishments in the competition. We became a team, a solid unit of men helping and encouraging each other to do their best.

By the way, remember that big Drill Sgt. who was always yelling and cussing at us? Well after the competition, he took me aside and told me how proud he was of me and that I was his favorite recruit. He said, "When others ridiculed you and made fun of your stature, you never stopped. You trained and pushed yourself to be the best you could be." Then he stopped and said that if I told anyone about his remarks to me he would kick my ---.

Another lesson from basic training was: What we are made of on the inside is more important than what we look like on the outside. We were taught how to look at others. Do we make quick judgments based on physical appearance? First Samuel 16:7 (NLT) gives us the proper way to see others: *The Lord doesn't see things the way you see them. People judge by outward appearance, but the Lord looks at the heart.*

How many marriages have failed because of the focus being on outward appearance? How many good employees have been overlooked due to their appearance or stature? We must all learn how to look at the character of others rather than their outside appearance.

After eight weeks of exhaustive physical and mental training, I was assigned to Fort Ord, California for my Advanced

Individual Training, a.k.a. "AIT." Since we were so close to Christmas, the Army gave us a 10-day leave before we went on to AIT. So I went home to Sharon and my family. We had 10 great days together. We celebrated Christmas and New Year's Eve. My hair was shaved off, and I looked like a tiny version of Arnold Schwarzenegger. Before you wonder why I would compare myself to Arnold, think of it this way, as a man I had the same number of muscles, in the same locations as Arnold.

Agree?! Okay, so mine were just a little smaller.

During my Christmas leave, Sharon and I spent as much time together as we could. While she was working, I was spending time with family and friends. Soon the day was approaching for me to go to Fort Ord for eight more weeks of training. I wondered where I would be assigned after AIT.

Sharon and I talked about getting married when I got my permanent assignment. Don't forget, I had been promised by my recruiting sergeant I would get a good assignment since I had volunteered for the draft. Sharon and I thought about moving to Germany or Italy. Why not dream for the best!

One of the Scriptures I know about today would have been a great help to me back in 1967. Philippians 4:6-7 says, *"Don't worry about anything; instead, pray about everything. Tell God what you need, and thank him for all he has done. Then you will experience God's peace, which exceeds anything we can understand. His peace will guard your hearts and minds as you live in Christ Jesus."* (NLT)

The day after we celebrated New Year's Eve, I boarded a plane for Fort Ord in northern California. My Advanced Individual Training would begin. One of the best things about AIT was the weekend. We were free to do anything we wanted after Monday through Friday training. So, I would leave on Friday at 5:00 PM. A greyhound bus would stop at Fort Ord and take me to the San Francisco airport. Then I would purchase a one-way standby ticket to Los Angeles. A convenient non-stop flight to Phoenix was not available. In Los Angeles, I would purchase a one-way standby ticket to Phoenix. When traveling, I always wore my army uniform. The airline clerks would make sure I never missed a flight. On several occasions they put me in 1st class. The Lord gave me favor then, even though I was not a believer.

About midnight, I would get to Phoenix. Sharon or my family would pick me up. Saturday night Sharon and I would go out. Then on Sunday at 10:00 PM I would catch a nonstop flight to San Francisco. Once again, it was a one-way standby ticket.

Arriving in San Francisco at 1:00 AM, I would catch a bus from the airport to Fort Ord. The bus would drop me off across the divided highway by the front gate.

Then, I needed to walk up the hill to my barracks. By the time I went to sleep it was around 3:00 A.M. You guessed it, that horrible bugle would play reveille at 5:30 A.M.

This process went on for about a month, until I asked Sharon to marry me. On February 10, 1967 we eloped to Las Vegas. Sharon and I were both 20 years old. In Nevada, the man had to be 21 years old, the woman could be 18 years old to get married. Therefore, I brought a notarized letter from my mother giving me permission to get married. Thanks, Mom.

Every weekend until my AIT was complete, I would fly home to Sharon. Only the Lord knew what would happen next.

By this time Vietnam was a raging war. We have proof today that President Johnson and Congress knew we could never win the war. General Westmoreland wanted at least another 200,000 troops on the ground. Fortunately, he was not successful with his request. We were approaching 500,000 boots on the ground in Vietnam. Thousands of American soldiers were dying every few months.

I was not aware that in a few weeks I would be assigned to Vietnam. The fear of being assigned to Vietnam was on the thoughts of almost every one of us being trained at Fort Ord. I have never met a person who was looking forward to going into a combat zone knowing they might be killed. The American soldier was fighting a war most people in the United States hated. American soldiers went to Vietnam for about a year. At the end of the year they could not wait to go back home.

The Vietcong, however, were willing to fight until every one of them were killed. They were fighting in their own country. Their leader Ho Chi Minh said they would fight until they ran out of children. Russia and China supplied our enemy with the best weapons needed to fight a jungle war. How could you defeat an enemy with such a commitment?

The people in America were protesting the war and began to see that it was a political nightmare. The decision was made by congress to continue the buildup of our forces in Vietnam. The United States of America was caught in a trap of lies, pride, arrogance, and deception. While all of this was happening we were sending tens of thousands of our young men and women to their death sentence.

Would I be one of these men?

LIFE APPLICATION

Training, conditioning, and becoming disciplined are vital to living any type of life. Hopefully, we all have received some type of discipline in our life. When we live with discipline we will desire to accept training and conditioning. The Bible tells us that we will profit when we accept discipline. When we submit to living a disciplined life we will just do what the Holy Spirit tells us to do.

After basic training I went back to Phoenix to be with my girl and family for Christmas 1966. Vietnam was not in my plans for our future. The recruiter had promised me a good assignment in Europe.

Fresh out of basic training with my Dad. I gained 24 pounds of muscle. How I miss my 28 inch waist.

"Lead me, Follow me, or get out of my way."

General Patton

CHAPTER 4

On My Way

At the age of 20, I was married to the most beautiful and loving girl I had ever known. My only regret is I wish we had married before I entered the military. Due to Sharon's family not wanting us to get married, we decided to wait and see if they would have a change of heart. We were ready, but they were not. We thought waiting a little longer might help them see we were deeply in love with each other. I knew that Sharon would be the woman with whom I would spend the rest of my life. We were willing to wait if it would bring peace to her family.

Peace did not come, so we decided to move forward with our plans to marry. We never imagined the first year of our marriage would face such great challenges. Thankfully, Sharon's parents accepted us years later.

About one week after our wedding, my orders were posted on the bulletin board at Fort Ord. Finally, my assignment to Europe would become a reality. As I looked at the 120 names on the board, I saw the names of guys who were going to Europe, Korea, and Hawaii. The print was small and my name was near the middle. There it was— David C. Friend US56909000 – assignment: Republic of Vietnam.

Wait a minute. What was that?

After looking again at the list of 120 guys, only two of us were going to Vietnam. His name was next to mine. It looked like someone must have closed their eyes and pinned the tail on the two of us.

My heart sank. What would I tell my bride, my family, my friends? Then I thought, *they made a mistake. I was trained in the area of personnel and did not have any combat training.* There was an asterisk by my name with a reference to check in with my commanding officer. Immediately, I went to his office and said three words to him, "Sir, why me?" He quickly said I would be okay, my training would have to include two weeks of Vietnam jungle training. My thought was, *Jungle training, are you kidding me?* The commanding officer, a.k.a. "CO" told me I had to be trained in jungle survival and combat awareness. But I had only two weeks left in my advanced individual training. How could I get ready to go to a war zone called Vietnam? They put me with all of those from Fort Ord who were going to Vietnam. We were taught how to keep our feet and rifles dry. They talked about the snakes, leeches, rats, and other dangers. So much for jungle training.

We were told we would probably be assigned to an infantry division as personnel specialists. We may be required to participate in all the patrols and maneuvers our company would undertake.

We were taught what we could eat and drink in a jungle environment. All of this seemed surreal. A sergeant who just returned from Vietnam in an infantry division warned us about punji sticks. The Vietcong would bury them in the ground. They were made of bamboo or wood with the end cut like a spear. The spearhead was covered with feces and or toxic chemicals. If stepped on, these sticks could pierce our rubber-soled boots. This weapon was intended to put our troops out of action for a few weeks. Pete, a close friend of mine, was a Marine stationed near Da Nang. He was unfortunate enough to step down on one of these sticks. He told me recently he is still experiencing discomfort from the wound.

I was saddened to discover the Vietcong would often use their children to set these sticks in tight places. Looking back on my preparation to go to Vietnam, with all the discussions about snakes, etc., I wish I had known of the Scripture verse found in Luke 10:19:

> "Look, I have given you authority over all the power of the enemy, and you can walk among snakes and scorpions and crush them. Nothing will injure you," (NLT)

After becoming a Christian I found it so encouraging to discover the Word of the Lord has a scriptural promise for anything we will face in our lives.

After two weeks of training, we were all certified to be ready to deal with the many dangers awaiting us in Vietnam. The Army's understanding of being certified and qualified to work and/or live in a combat zone in a jungle was a little ridiculous.

However, President Johnson wanted a massive buildup of our military in Vietnam. Evidently, it did not matter to him if we were prepared to go. Think of the number of troops like me who had as little as a few months of military training. From the time I volunteered for the draft to the day I arrived in Vietnam, I had less than 90 days of actual training days. Weekends were not training days. This included my eight weeks of basic, six weeks of AIT, and 10 days for Vietnam duty.

We all felt like we were going through a crash course in survival. My life was in a whirlwind of confusion, doubt, and fear. The only good thing happening in my life was being newly married to my dream wife, Sharon. Preparing for Vietnam was difficult. But, preparing to tell my bride about it was even more difficult. We had been married for only a week, but we had been dating for nearly a year and a half. I called Sharon and told her the bad news but assured her I would be okay. I wish I had believed what I told her. The weekend I flew back to see Sharon and my family was extremely difficult. Not being a follower of Jesus Christ, it was impossible for me to understand the promises Jesus gives to His followers. The peace Jesus spoke of was not in me.

Sharon met me at the airport. Although I was always positive, Sharon knew this was different. It was obvious I was deeply troubled about Vietnam. To her, I must have looked like a deer looking at headlights as I walked up to her. As we walked through the airport we were very silent. When we got into the car she started to cry. I had a tough time seeing her in tears. Back in 1967 men were not supposed to cry.

We drove back to my parent's home where we would stay for the weekend. Everything was moving fast around us. We were filled with questions. We watched the news on television and read everything we could about Vietnam. I remember calling Sharon one day while I was finishing up at Fort Ord. Trying to find something positive, I told her because we were married and I was going into a combat zone, combined with my promotion to E-3 Private First Class, my pay would increase to $125 a month. We were set financially. Sharon did not get much comfort from my pay increase.

During our conversation, she told me we were going to have a baby. I told her it was wonderful news. She did not think the timing was all that wonderful. Sharon would be pregnant while I was in Vietnam.

As I look back on those days, I thank the Lord for helping us deal with everything we faced. Even though we had not yet become Christians, we believed in prayer. We prayed, she prayed, I prayed, my family prayed. The Lord was hearing about our situation 24/7.

The Army gave me a 20-day leave before I went to Vietnam. When I left Fort Ord, I was given orders to be at Travis Air Force Base by mid-March 1967. I don't remember the exact date. What I do remember is how my new bride found us a little furnished apartment we could rent for a couple of weeks. What an amazing yet challenging time it was in our marriage. Although I was going into a combat zone, we were able to focus on each other. We went to church. I was baptized in the Lutheran Church and we started to pray together.

It seemed like only hours had passed before I needed to pack up and head for Vietnam. My family was great to us. Sharon's family had moved to Florida and we had very little contact with them. Although I love my family, the love I felt for Sharon was overwhelming. There she was, trying to smile and keep it together as we headed for the airport. On the way, she looked at me and said, "Promise me you will come back from Vietnam in one piece just like you are today." I said something like, "I promise you, I guarantee you I will be just fine."

With my expecting wife and family at the terminal, I walked up the steps to fly away again. Although we were not Christians, we knew beyond a shadow of a doubt God would protect me. We knew I would be back and my wife and child would be there for me.

That night I flew to Travis Air Force Base, located 52 miles from San Francisco. There I met about 100 men going to Vietnam. We spent the night at the air base. Early the next day we boarded a four-engine prop airplane. Most of the Army guys I knew flew to Vietnam on a 707 jet. Being on a four-engine prop, my group felt we were traveling in slow motion. It took us nearly 12 hours to fly to Hawaii in a strong head wind.

Then, we flew to Midway Island, Guam, and Tan Son Nhut Air Base near Saigon. All totaled, it took over two days to get to Vietnam.

It was a grind, but then we were told our time in Vietnam started when we boarded in California. That meant I was in my third day of Vietnam duty when we arrived. Sometimes it's the little things that help a lot.

My friend Pete, who was a Marine said, "You Army guys had it made. You got to fly there. The Marines went over on a ship." Pete was in the first landing of Marines in 1965. (Thank you for your service, Pete. Welcome home.)

During our long flights, I got to know some of the guys I thought I would possibly serve with in Vietnam. But after our arrival, it was less than a few hours before I discovered all those I had just met, I would never see again. They were assigned all over South Vietnam.

I thank the Lord for all those I met on the plane. I hoped I had said something encouraging to them. It is sad to think I was not a Christian and I could not share the promises Jesus has for those who accept Him.

LIFE APPLICATION

We are all on our way to something. Some may be learning a new career. Others may be moving to another state or into a new relationship. There are those who are on the road to success or failure. Regardless of the stage of the journey we are on, we must keep our eyes on our desired destination. Another way to say it is, "Keep your eyes on the prize."

New trainees on their way to Vietnam. Some would not return. Others came back with physical and or emotional scars. We flew over on a four-engine prop commercial airline. It took over two days to get there. Our first stop was in Hawaii.

"Don't be afraid to see what you see."

RONALD REAGAN

SECTION II
During Vietnam

CHAPTER 5

Entering the Country

Our flight was over. We all walked down the steps of our air-craft at the Tan Son Nhut Air Base in Saigon, Vietnam. As we walked across the tarmac, we noticed a tremendous amount of activity. The C – 130 Hercules aircraft were being loaded and unloaded. As we walked closer to one of these aircraft, we saw a couple of dozen large dark bags lying on the tarmac. Turning to the guy next to me, I asked him, "What is in those bags?" Since this was not his first walk across the airport, he looked at me and said, "They have dead soldiers in them, we call them body bags."

Immediately, about half of us turned to look in that direction. Some of us stopped for a brief moment and stared in disbelief. Body bags containing someone's son, daughter, husband, father. "Body bags," who came up with that? But when you think about it, what else can you call them? All of these soldiers had paid the ultimate price. These men and women gave their life so others may live. John 15:13 reads, *"There is no greater love than to lay down one's life for one's friends."*(NLT)

This was the first time I asked myself, *Why is this necessary? Who decides who lives or who dies?* While these body bags laid on the tarmac, it was just another day in Vietnam. Planes taxied by them, trucks passed quickly, and a new batch of replacements walked by in disbelief. At that moment I decided I would not return in one of those bags. I asked God to help me get through this next year. It was unexplainable, but a sense of peace passed over me.

Another aircraft called a C-123 was being filled with some chemicals. I asked the guy who had been there before what type of chemicals were being loaded. He quickly responded, "That's called agent orange." He told me it could save my life someday. It was sprayed on the foliage to kill as much vegetation as possible. This would give the Vietcong fewer places to hide. At the time I did not know one day I would discover that Agent Orange would become my worst enemy.

As we loaded up on a green bus (not Eco-friendly) to take us to the 90th Replacement Battalion, our minds were filled with thoughts of fear, death, and uncertainty. The bus had heavily screened windows, designed to keep anyone from tossing in a hand grenade.

We have all heard it said you get only one chance to make a first impression. Well, my first impression of this place was embedded in my memory for a lifetime. The bus drove briskly down the streets in the direction of my next assignment. The people in Vietnam lived like nothing I had ever seen before. Most of the houses looked like they were about to fall over. Some of the doorways and exterior walls were covered with flattened Coke and beer cans. They had been sewn together with wire or string. This place was filthy. The smell was overwhelming. The odor caused me to choke as through I was going to vomit. I noticed only a few dogs running in the streets. Later, I discovered that dog meat had been and continues to be a favorite of the Vietnamese.

The streets were in terrible condition. We could see various types of transportation being utilized. Bicycles, motorized and manual, were everywhere. Vespas, scooters, small buses, carts, motorcycles, and rickshaws were moving in every direction. Some of the taxis were large tricycles with one wheel in front and two on the back, enabling them to carry a small, open cage-type box. This is where the passengers would sit or hang on the outside edge of the box. We could see as many as six or seven people attached in one way or another in or on the taxis.

The thing that shocked me the most was the open sewage in the streets. A small ditch ran along the edges of the road. The men, women, and children would relieve themselves in plain view in these ditches. You guessed it — both numbers. This is when I wondered about what type of toilets we would be using. Within an hour or so I would become familiar with the toilet facilities I would be using for the next year. Oh well, let's move on.

To the people of Vietnam; war was a way of life. From generation to generation they were in conflict with other countries. War had taken a toll on the lives and morals of everyone. What we take for granted in the USA was an unknown luxury for the Vietnamese people.

In about a half an hour our green buses were pulling into the 90th Replacement Battalion in Long Bien. As the name implies, this was a facility where up to 2500 replacements, both men and women, would wait for their assignment in Vietnam. The compound was primarily dirt and gravel. A small lagoon of standing water was near the center. Next to the lagoon was a helicopter pad. A wire fence circled the compound with guard bunkers stationed about 50 to 75 yards apart. The bus dropped us off in a large dirt area where the troops would gather daily to hear their names called out for their assignments.

Single- and two-story wood buildings housed the permanent and temporary troops. The sides of the buildings looked like opened venetian blinds. They were built to help air circulate through the structures. They had poured concrete floors with a very rough textured finish. At first I wondered why they did not smooth out the concrete floors. But at least we had some concrete to walk on. Most of our combat soldiers lived and slept on dirt and mud. They would have loved our rough-finished concrete floors. All of the buildings had sandbags stacked about five feet high surrounding the exterior walls.

My first question was, *Are these good or bad accommodations compared to everywhere else?* Soon I discovered the word "accommodations" did not always apply to those serving in Vietnam.

The thought of being at home with Sharon in our little apartment with no air conditioning sounded wonderful. I would never complain again about my living conditions in hot Phoenix, Arizona. Then I thought, *What is my beautiful wife doing? How is she feeling? It would be so wonderful to talk to her.* However, cell phones and the internet had not even been invented. The only way to communicate would be by letters and tape recordings. This was going to be a year with men I had never met. A year without my wife and family. My prayer was, "Lord, make it go quickly."

Looking back, it was a day filled with confusion. All of us have lived in moments of confusion, fear, and doubt. After becoming a Christian, I have found comfort in the words of the apostle Paul in 2 Timothy 1:7, *"For God has not given us a spirit of fear and timidity, but of power, love, and self-discipline."* (NLT) May these words give you comfort as you face your trials.

So this was South Vietnam. What was so important about a place that had nothing to offer their people? Why was our country willing to sacrifice the lives of so many of our young men and women? Was this going to help our country? We have all heard of these questions being asked by the people of America. To this day we see videos of protests in the streets of our country concerning the Vietnam War. But, how did our soldiers feel about this war? Were they aware of the reasons why they were even there? In the last chapter of this book I have a list of what I call, "The Whys of Vietnam." Some of those reading my words may have their own opinions of what Vietnam was all about. However, with all due respect, may I suggest that opinions are never equal to actual experience. Those who served in Vietnam and their loved ones are the only ones who must be listened to; so we will never again become involved in another Vietnam in the future.

LIFE APPLICATION

Change is said to be the only thing we all must experience. When some face change they run in the opposite direction, while others are drawn to change. Change is always a time of growth. Good or bad, change causes us to increase our understanding of what others experience. When you face a change in your life, look for the potential for growth in that change.

Typical home in the city of Bien Hoa. At least this one would keep out some of the weather.

This small taxi would carry many Vietnamese. Some would hang on the outside edges of the taxi.

The streets would become inundated with various forms of transportation. This was a very light day of activity.

South Vietnamese and U.S. troops would work together in the same complex.

"Your mind is your prison when you focus on your fear."

TIM FARGO, AUTHOR

CHAPTER 6

Formation Call

The Tech Sergeant who greeted us as we got off the bus told us we should take a break and find a place to store our duffel bags. These were large green bags filled with our fatigues, boots, and personal gear. He told us a two-story barracks would be our temporary quarters at the 90th Replacement Battalion. A bunk on the upper floor of one of the barracks in the back edge of the compound became my new temporary home.

Several of the men I met went to the same barracks with me to talk about what we may be facing next. The discussion between all of the new replacements was typical of young men. When do we eat? What is there to do? Where are the ladies? Do they have beer? We sat around talking until a loud siren-type sound could be heard everywhere. What does that siren mean? Someone questioned. Are we under attack? Is it time to eat? One of the men who had been at the 90th for a day or so said the siren was our call to assemble in the formation area where the buses had dropped us off. As I jumped up to go to the formation, another man said, "Don't worry your name will not be called for three or four days." He warned us if we went to the formation and our name was not called out, we would be assigned to do kitchen duty or cleanup details. One of these details was burning the waste from the latrines, a.k.a. outhouses. Another guy asked if we would get in trouble by not going to the formation. The comment was made, "What are they going to do; send us to Vietnam?" That became the common response for us when we faced possible discipline.

At first I thought I better go. Then, why not just stay here? Instantly, I felt a still, quiet inner voice say to me. "Go to the formation." My mind said, "Stay." However, the quiet voice said "Go."

Years later when I had become a Christian, I read about a still, quiet voice speaking to Elisha after his victory over the prophets of Baal. The Bible tells us it was like a whisper from God. That day I felt a whisper from somewhere or some person or spirit. At the time, I struggled with what action to take. Thankfully the whisper won the battle for my actions. I ran out the barracks toward the formation area.

A loud, angry voice over the speaker was saying someone's name. Here was a large group of men standing in formation and waiting for their names to be called out. The angry voice over the loudspeaker said, "For the third and final time, will PFC David C. Friend number US 56909000 report to the front."

Instantly, I froze and started to think the worst. They caught me, I'm in trouble. What have I done? Now, they will send me to the worst place in the world. But then I thought, This is the worst place in the world.

Without further self-examination of my circumstances, I ran up to the front of the formation to meet my doom. One of the cadre (a guy who worked at the 90th) said to me, "Are you PFC David C. Friend?" My response was, "Yes, what did I do wrong?" He said, "You have not done anything wrong except almost miss out on a great opportunity." Following him to the headquarters building he told me to wait outside. Then he added, "The personnel sergeant of the 90th wants to see you."

Still nervous and wondering what this is all about, I waited for this so-called opportunity. Shortly, I was ordered to stand inside the headquarters building. They had me wait for the sergeant in charge. His name escapes me. We have tried unsuccessfully to retrieve that sergeant's name. Let's just call him "Sarge."

Sarge walked in and told me to sit down. His first question was, "Is that your real last name? Friend?" Proudly, my answer was, "Yes, sergeant." Then he told me, "One of the men reviewing the list of new replacements saw your name and sent me your file." Sarge was from Ohio and noticed it was my birthplace. Then he said, "I love the Ohio State buckeyes." Quickly, I responded, "So do I." His next question was a life-changing one for me. "How would you like to stay here at the 90th for your year in country?" Without thinking I asked if that was good. What else is out there? He started to laugh and tried to explain the good, the bad, and the ugly details of assignments in Vietnam.

Sarge was a great guy; he must've stood six feet four and weighed at least 260 pounds. With very kind words he said something like this: "I can send you almost anywhere I want. Saigon to Da Nang, an infantry company in the Mekong Delta, or to an administrative position in Cam Ranh Bay (that was a beach)." He continued, "If I had my choice of any place in Vietnam to be assigned it would be right here at the 90th." Then Sarge said, "I need a personnel specialist, you are from Ohio and have a great last name. Would you join us at the 90th?" Sarge went on to say, "This place is not perfect, you will go on patrols in the Long Binh area. You will spend many nights on guard duty in a bunker on the perimeter of this compound. However, we are like a family, and I will be your dad." After his explanation I accepted and became cadre at the 90th.

Thank you, Lord for the whisper. Thank you, Dad for my last name. Thank you, Mom for giving birth to me in Ohio.

Allow me to speak to you about how my experience in Vietnam can help you today. To be very honest, I felt a little guilty. I had a good assignment. Later, I would feel guilty to send thousands of men into severe combat areas.

Have you been confused about a decision you need to make? Are you in doubt about your job, your future, your purpose in life?

Try the following steps to hear the still, quiet whisper from the Lord.

1) Get alone and speak to the Lord.
2) Meditate on God's word. Find a scripture that speaks to your heart.
3) Get around other believers who are positive and encouraging.
4) Settle down in a good church that teaches from God's Word.
5) Ask the Holy Spirit to reveal his direction for your life.

I was not a follower of Jesus Christ when I served in Vietnam. However, I know the Lord sent his Holy Spirit to whisper into my heart what was the right thing to do. He can do the same for you today.

As you will discover the 90th Replacement Battalion was a pretty good assignment for a clerical specialist. One of the struggles I had was to send men to difficult assignments. The thousands of personnel files we forwarded to various locations in South Vietnam had a person connected to them. Command would request men to be sent into the Mekong Delta to replace those who were going home or had been killed in action. A sense of responsibility gripped me. Would these soldiers be killed or permanently injured? Will I be responsible for lost lives?

Only the Lord knows what happened to the men our battalion sent all over South Vietnam. The older I get the more I wonder about those men. If it wasn't for the Word of God I would still be struggling with those thoughts. Proverbs 3:5 told me to, "Trust in the Lord with all your heart; do not depend on your own understanding."(NLT) My prayer for you today, for whatever you are facing is to allow the words from Proverbs 3:5 to give you comfort and peace.

LIFE APPLICATION

I believe the Holy Spirit will whisper to your heart about the decisions you may be facing. Be still, and listen to the quiet voice. The Bible tells us the Lord is a very present help in times of trouble; He wants to help you today. Take a moment and listen for God's voice. If you do not hear the still, quiet voice today then continue to listen until you do. That voice may speak to you through someone else or while you read His word.

Routine work day at the 90th Replacement Battalion. My living quarters with sandbags to protect from mortar attack.

The rain was constant and humidity was relentless.

Typical Vietnamese working woman, seemingly paying little attention to U.S. military traffic.

"Blessed are the flexible, for they shall not be bent out of shape."

ANONYMOUS

Assignments

My first night as a member of the 90th Replacement Battalion was very restless. "Cadre," those permanently working at the 90th, were assigned to the single-story barracks near the 90th headquarters building. The barracks were made of wood with a corrugated metal roof. The floor was concrete. Whoever poured the concrete must have missed the training on how to put a smooth finish on the floor. Small, sharp stones stood up out of the concrete. It was extremely rough and uneven. Some who served in Vietnam could say, "At least you had a concrete floor."

One night soon after my assignment to the 90th , I remember waking up feeling something was in my bunk with me. We used mosquito netting and let it hang down around the bunk to keep the insects out. However, little did I realize letting the netting fall down to the floor provided a ladder for some of the other crawling creatures. Something ran across my leg, made its way onto my stomach, and rested on my chest. My eyes were closed but I knew I had to open them. What was in bed with me? Was it a snake? Was it a rat? Well, I had to find out. As I looked at my chest I could see the eyes and mouth of a huge rat. Quickly, I sat up and the rat decided to run up on top of my head. As if that was not bad enough, I could feel its tail wagging over my neck and ear.

Since I was trained in hand-to-hand combat and had a crash course in jungle survival training, I did what came natural. I screamed like a little girl and flew out of my bunk onto the floor. That is when I discovered how sharp the stones in our poorly finished concrete floors were. As soon as I hit the floor I screamed out again. This time from the many cuts and abrasions on my bare feet. One of the men who was trying to sleep cussed at me and turned on the overhead light bulb. When the light came on you could see a couple of dozen rats running for protection. Now I understood why we were told never to leave any food out at night.

My ego was damaged when I realized many of the men in our barracks were laughing at my experience. Still others were cursing and telling me to turn off the light. So much for team compassion. With my bare feet cut and bleeding, I crawled back into my bunk. This time I was careful to stuff the netting under my three inch thick mattress to keep this event from happening again.

This would not be my only experience with rats in Vietnam. Learning to sleep with the rats crawling at night became no big deal. With the conditions our combat troops faced daily, I felt blessed to have a roof over my head and a bed.

During the day, I was assigned to process the records of those arriving at the 90th. We processed over 300,000 assignments for both men and women during my year. Daily, the United States Army Republic of Vietnam, a.k.a. USARV, in

Saigon would send instructions on how many they needed to be sent to other locations in Vietnam. USARV would order our battalion to send troops, based on their MOS, to various divisions, battalions, and companies all over South Vietnam. The acronym "MOS" (military occupational specialty) was to identify specific training specialties. My MOS was 71B20, personnel specialist. An 11B20 was infantry. A 12D was a driver, 12K plumber, 13M rocket launching, 13T field artillery. There are nearly 200 such MOS designations in the Army and Marines.

As I looked through the files of thousands of men I thought of how blessed I was to be assigned to the 90th. I was selected to join the 90th because of being born in Ohio and my last name was Friend. Since I was blessed, I thought maybe I could help someone else. If I came across someone from Ohio or Arizona I would try to help them in some way.

Until Vietnam, I had never been a person who prayed. Even though I was raised in a Baptist church and went to Sunday school, church, and summer vacation Bible school, I almost never prayed. However, Vietnam made me think of calling out to a Higher Power often. All my life I've heard you will never find an atheist in a foxhole. That started to make sense. So almost every night I would pray something like this: "If there is a God out there, I need you. God help me through this and I will go to church." This was not a very deep theological prayer, but it came from my heart.

As I said in chapter six, I felt a tremendous burden for the thousands of men whom I had a part in sending all over Vietnam. Some would face possible death or injury. As a Christian today, I understand it was the Holy Spirit of God who gave me such a burden for others and their welfare. After coming home from Vietnam, there have been times when I felt sorrow for the men I may have sent to an early death. The Lord has lifted that burden from me.

Processing files was my daytime work. The Army gave me other assignments that were just as important. Without a doubt, my most difficult assignment was to work out of a perimeter guard bunker at night. If my memory serves me correctly, we were responsible for the security of approximately 2500 unarmed soldiers a day at the 90th. These men were there for a few days awaiting their permanent assignment. Although most of the cadre of the 90th were trained in administrative jobs, we were also responsible for providing protection for our new replacements. There were about 200 who worked at the 90th permanently. In addition to our clerical work, we were the first line of defense from any military attack by the Vietcong.

Our compound had perimeter guard bunkers set up approximately 50-75 yards apart. Many of us were assigned to be on guard duty at night. Usually we were assigned to the same bunker nightly. That way we were familiar with the vegetation, sounds, and activity in our area. My station was in a low-lying, swamp-like area on the opposite side of the compound from the headquarters. My time on perimeter was usually in the middle of the night. I was surprised I went out to the perimeter alone each night. We were told two men were supposed to go together in order to protect each other's backs. However in my area, those who went out on the perimeter had to go alone.

When we would walk out to replace someone, we were given a new code word each night in order to identify who we were to the one we were replacing.

Something else that confused me was how a guard bunker was constructed. The structure was built higher than the area we guarded. On most nights, I could see the silhouette of the guy in the next bunker. Think about it, would you want the outline of your body at night to be seen for 50 yards in every direction? Most of the men I knew would not sit in the bunker on a moonlit night. They would find a place next to the bunker that seemed a little safer.

As the guy I replaced would go back into the main compound, I would get myself set for the hours of being alone. My number one thought was, *Is this the night I would die? Would a sniper pick me off? Would a Vietcong sneak up on me and end my life?*

I probably watched too many war movies as a kid. Because of those movies, I would sit with my M-14 rifle across my chest with the barrel guarding my neck. My thought was this would keep a cord or wire from choking me. Sounds silly now, but it made sense to me then. By the way, I never told any of my friends this technique.

Somehow I don't think I was any different than most of the young men in Vietnam. This was a new world to us. After all, we were part of the Disneyland generation. The majority of us had never fired a military rifle or used a knife against someone else. We were from the baby boomer generation. Rock 'n roll, high school dances, and the typical American family was our background. Many of us were in the same situation, college draftees, high school dropouts, newly married, some expecting a child. Most were between the ages of 18 and 21. It is no wonder so many young men and women who served in Vietnam or other wars are dealing with Post Traumatic Stress Disorder, a.k.a. PTSD.

When I returned home from Vietnam I was not told PTSD could be a problem for me someday. Like most of those who return home from serving in a combat zone, I experienced months of nightmares. Some of my PTSD lasted for years.

There was never a time when the Veterans Administration inquired about my adjustment to civilian life. How many Vietnam veterans were dealing with issues they could not understand? Evidently, very few in the VA were concerned about the mental wellbeing of returning vets.

What I remember most about Vietnam was the hours of feeling alone and being afraid of dying all by myself. The worst place for that was on perimeter guard duty. On a rainy night, and we had a lot of those, I would sit in my poncho (a covering) and hear noises or see something that was not there. Rats and an occasional snake would break up my solitude.

Had I known Jesus as my Lord I could have asked him for peace. If only I would've known Philippians 4:6-7,

> "Don't worry about anything; instead, pray about everything. Tell God what you need, and thank Him for all He has done. Then you will experience God's peace, which exceeds anything we can understand. His peace will guard your hearts and minds as you live in Christ Jesus." (NLT)

To this day, I pray that Scripture. Every night before I sleep those words give me peace. How about you? Do you need peace about something in your life? May I encourage you to make this passage of scripture part of your day?

One of the assignments I questioned was being called on to deliver personnel files to the Saigon headquarters in the middle of the night. This happened several times during my tour of duty. It would be 2:00 a.m. and my commanding officer would order two of us to get a Jeep and drive up Highway One to US-ARV headquarters. While transporting these files, we would see enemy tracer rounds being fired in our direction. It was the middle of the night and we were the only vehicle on the road. We assumed some officer wanted the files in his office by daybreak. Why not wait until daylight when it was safer? However, when you are in the military you don't ask why. Reminds me of what we were told in basic training: "Don't ask why just do it or die!"

Looking back at what we experienced in Vietnam, it is my opinion we had no business fighting that war. American soldiers were not mentally prepared to fight the type of enemy we encountered. Besides, the American people did not support us. We were there because our president told us to go. The Vietcong and North Vietnamese Army were there because it was their home. They lived off of their land for hundreds of years. They knew how to fight in a jungle. Our military battle plans worked great in WWII; however, they would not in Vietnam. In the early years of the war most Americans thought our president knew what he was doing. They believed he would not put our soldiers in harm's way without justification.

When I arrived in Vietnam I believed we would win this war. After only a few months in country, I started to question why we were there and if we had any chance of winning. The Vietnamese did not welcome American soldiers. The Vietcong referred to us as raiders or bandits. Before we went there, they did not want the French in their country. Now, they did not want us, nor did they trust us.

The Vietcong felt they would never lose. We began to feel that we would never win. The North Vietnamese Army leaders said if we could not win with 500,000 troops, we could never win.

The Russians and Chinese kept the NVA and Vietcong well supplied with AK-47 rifles and artillery. They were committed to spreading communism to South Vietnam, Laos, and Cambodia. We were foolish to believe if we killed tens of thousands it would break their will to fight. At the same time, the NVA and Vietcong were willing to lose 100 of their men in exchange for killing only a few of ours. How can you defeat an enemy with that kind of commitment? The hearts of the men I served with felt after one year they would be out of there. We were fighting an undefeatable enemy. Why stay? Let's just go home.

With all of that happening, I would talk to the God who I did not know personally. Often, I would promise Him if He would protect me, I would go to a church service somewhere.

The person I missed most was Sharon. I wrote to her daily. How I wished I could hear her voice. One day I came across a poem. It was entitled "My Wife." The author is unknown to me. When I read it, something touched my heart. As you read it, try to think of the thousands of husbands who have experienced war far from home. From the Revolutionary War to the Afghanistan War many have faced the emptiness of having a wife far away.

My Wife
My wife is home, so far away,
I love her more each passing day,
I left her behind in misery
too fight for freedom in this country.
I had no choice in coming here
leaving her lonely, and full of tears.
I'll make it up to her one day;
until I do, I'll hope and pray.
I pray to God that she is safe.
In her, I trust, in love, in faith.
I'll be back with her at home one day,
but until then, my days are gray.
So please, my Lord, so high above.
Protect this girl, this girl I love.

That poem told me God loved Sharon and I. I knew how much I loved Sharon and how much I missed her.

Looking back, I can see God loved me even though I did not love Him. All I wanted was something from Him. Now I can see I serve the God who protected me when I needed Him.

God loves all of us. He loves us so much that he gave His Son's life for us. Do you need God to help you today? Seek Him, speak to Him. Our God is a very present help in times of trouble. (See Psalm 46:1.) He loves you and has a plan for your life. Give your heart to Him and He will never leave you or forsake you. (See Hebrews 13:5.)

LIFE APPLICATION

Everyone will face assignments in life. Going to school, starting a career, getting married, becoming a parent are all assignments. How we deal with these assignments will determine our successes or failures. When new assignments come into our lives we must look for the opportunities in them.

Headquarters for the 90th. We protected 2000-2500 replacement troops with 200 permanent men.

A small pond with a stream flowed through our compound.
My guard station was near this area.

Outside of the city of Bien Hoa, a prisoner of war camp held questionable and convicted war criminals.

The French once occupied Vietnam and their architecture was seen throughout the country. This was a vacant catholic church.

"A friend when in need is a faithful friend."

VIETNAMESE PROVERB

CHAPTER 8

Relationships in Vietnam

When I first arrived in Vietnam, I did not know a single person very well. With the exception of a couple of guys I sat beside on the airplane, I could not tell you the first name of anyone. My first contact with these guys was at Travis Air Force Base in California, when my name was called to board my flight. Some of the men were there with a friend from the states. The military had a Buddy Enlistment option. Guys could join together and go through basic and advanced training as a team. That would have been good for me, except for the requirement to sign up for four years. As a volunteer for the draft, my commitment was only two years. It was difficult for me to see why anything longer than two years was necessary.

Everyone and everything was new to me. It was the same for the majority of us in Vietnam. Like my dad, I found it easy to meet new people. However, this was different. All of us had to adjust to new acquaintances, a new country, a new culture, and do it in a war zone. In addition to that we knew any friendship would be over in a year when we all went back to the states.

We did not know what the Vietnamese would be like. Our training taught us to be careful of the civilians we would come in contact with. It would be difficult to determine who the Vietcong were from the civilians. Approximately 40% of the civilians we would meet were supportive of the Vietcong. Of course we did not know that when we served there. Even the children could be our enemy. The shop or bar owner may be working with the Vietcong.

So, here we are in Vietnam. Sometimes we would drive through the streets of Saigon or Bien Hoa in an open Jeep. We passed by thousands of people who seemed to be going about life as though nothing unusual was happening. Even with hundreds of American trucks and jeeps driving through their cities daily, they acted like they did not even notice us. When we drove out of the city and into the open areas we saw Vietnamese farming and working with their livestock. The photos we saw in training were coming to life. This was one of my most surreal experiences in life.

What were these people thinking as hundreds of new American troops drove down their streets? Almost none of them even looked in our direction or acted like they cared whether we were there or not. When we arrived in Vietnam, not a single person even waved as a sign of welcome. The people of Vietnam had seen war and foreigners go through their land for hundreds of years. They must of thought American troops would come and go just like everyone else.

North and South Vietnam were at war. That was nothing unusual for them. The south wanted a loose form of democracy and the north wanted communism. But in reality, the people of Vietnam just wanted to raise a family and be at peace. They were willing to do that under any type of government. That is hard for us to understand because we have always lived in a free country.

Anyone from America had to feel sorry for the way the Vietnamese civilians lived. Houses looked like any storm would destroy them. Did the Vietnamese have any hope for the future? Did they feel they would ever live in peace? Was there a desire to improve their way of life?

During my time there I wondered if I would ever get to know any of these people. Would I get a chance to talk to the young people about America and living in freedom? We saw people who needed help with every aspect of life. We felt they needed medical help, an education, and sanitary living conditions. We were there to help them in all of these areas. But, did they really want what we thought they needed? How many wanted us to just go away and leave them alone? How many hated us?

How many would kill us if they were given the opportunity? How I wish I knew then what I know now about being a child of God. Jesus loved the Vietnamese just as much as he loved me. My prayer today is Christianity will expand through Vietnam. Then they will know peace and freedom.

Once I settled into living at the 90th, I discovered cleaning the mud from my boots and keeping my bunk area free of mud would be a challenge. About 30 men lived together in our barracks, a.k.a. "hooch." We all had the same problem with mud. One of the men told me a Vietnamese woman was coming into our hooch daily to clean up all the mud on the floors. In addition, she would clean the mud off our boots. For only three dollars a month she would do all that work. He told me the lady is known as our mama san. By the way she was not a prostitute. Our mama san received about $100 total every month from our 30 men giving her about $3.00 each. With that she could live in a home and support her family. She had 10 children and looked to be about 40 years old. She was very pleasant but spoke only a few English words. She was the first Vietnamese person I had ever met. This war helped her support her family.

It was almost impossible to communicate with the Vietnamese people. During my entire year in Vietnam I met only a couple of Vietnamese who spoke English. Most of those I met knew only a few of our words. Those who owned small shops or a bar could speak just enough English to make a sale. Looking back, I wish I would've known how to communicate with the civilians of Vietnam. Today my biggest regret is that I was not a believer in Jesus Christ in 1967-68. Because I was not a Christian, I was not able to share my faith with anyone, even those with whom I served.

Most of the men I knew were great guys. We had similar backgrounds. These men were 19-21 years old. They came from everywhere in the United States.

Because of the short amount of time we would spend together in Vietnam, it was difficult to build any kind of relationships. We did not come over together as a group like the Marines, or like some of the other army units. We were a bunch of guys who were sent there to fill a single vacant position. Guys were coming in and out of the 90th on a daily basis. The permanent men rotated out based on the completion of their year in country. Usually I kept to myself. My focus was to stay alert on guard duty and play it as safe as I could every day.

I had a number of acquaintances but only one real friend. His name was John. He was from New Shrewsbury, New Jersey. Like me, he was married and his wife was expecting their first child. John and I hit it off immediately. We liked to play pinochle and enjoyed the same type of music. The first day we talked to each other he said he hated white guys. He was an African American and of course I was white. When I told him I planned to stay white he grinned. He looked at me with anger and said, "White people cannot be trusted, but you don't act white."

As a pastor for 20 years, I ministered to white, black, Asian, and Hispanic people. Every once in a while, one of our black members would tell me I was a black preacher trapped in a white man's body. Maybe John liked me because he saw a little bit of a black man's heart in me. I think John liked me because my favorite female singer was Aretha Franklin. My favorite male singer was Chuck Berry. Both were extremely successful black artists in the 60s. Whatever it was, John and I became the best of friends. We always had each other's backs. We talked about our wives and future children. John had the same type of church background as mine, Southern Baptist. Like me, John never confessed to being a born-again Christian. We believed in prayer but never prayed together. Today I wish I could've been a Christian brother to John. When I returned home I made several attempts to locate John, but all were unsuccessful. Hopefully he has lived a good life and has accepted Jesus as his Lord and Savior. Thank you, John, for being my friend during a time in my life when I needed one the most.

In life we all have a number of acquaintances. Sometimes, we may call them our friends. However, a true friend is a friend forever. As a pastor, I discovered women have more friends than men. Women like to build relationships with the ladies they know. Men prefer to experience activities together and call it relationship. Children will call anyone a friend even if they have just met them for the first time.

The Word of God has a deeper definition of being a friend. What can we do if we don't have a close friend in our lives? In the book of Proverbs chapter 18, verse 24 we read, *"There are 'friends' who pretend to be friends, but there is a friend who sticks closer than a brother."* (TLB)

We must decide to be a friend before we can have one. My one true friend in Vietnam was there for me whenever I needed him. In the same way, I was there for him. John went home to his wife and family and I went home to mine. Without either one of us having faith in or a relationship with God, He sent His influence of friendship to help us during our time of need. I believe the Lord can do that for anyone. There will always be someone in our lives to whom we can be a friend. We will never experience true friendship with others until we decide to pursue friendship with the Lord. Jesus wants to call you His friend. But first, we must become friends to Him.

LIFE APPLICATION

A relationship can be defined as having a personal connection with someone else. It requires us to be transparent. Many individuals are afraid to be transparent because it makes them vulnerable to being hurt emotionally. We must never allow prior relationship failures to rob us of potentially wonderful future friendships.

We had a helicopter pad in the middle of our compound. It was used to bring in military dignitaries and civilians. Huey's and huge Chinook's were common.

The sound of Huey helicopters were at times pounded into our thoughts. Any Vietnam Vet will never forget that thumping sound.

My best friend John was from New Jersey. Like Sharon and I he was married and his wife was expecting their first child.

This Vietnamese woman worked 5 days a week cleaning the mud off of our boots and in our barracks. She received $3 a month from every G.I. This supported her family and provided a real house in the city.

"It's the unexpected that changes our lives."

Anonymous

CHAPTER 9

Expect the Unexpected

The Army tried to train us for what to expect in Vietnam. They taught us how to defend ourselves. We were told how to survive for a few days in the jungle. My training included how to deal with the civilian population. Some of our training came from Vietnam veterans who had experienced just about anything that could possibly happen to us. During my time in Vietnam it became common to experience the unexpected. Here are a few of my experiences. Somehow I hope they will prepare you for the unexpected in your life. Your experiences will not be like the ones I experienced, but learning to expect the unexpected will be of value no matter what we face in life.

Upon my arrival in Vietnam, I began to experience some unexpected dental issues. As a kid I had a lot of cavities. Due to my love of candy, combined with my poor dental hygiene, it seemed like every time I went to the dentist they would find a new cavity. The sound of a dentist drill still disturbs me.

Because of my previous dental problems, the unexpected was about to happen. Shortly after checking into the 90th I discovered I had an abscessed tooth that required immediate attention. The abscessed tooth became so painful that a trip to a dentist was required. Sick bay would be my first stop. They referred me to a dental infirmary that took care of emergencies. As I walked into this tent-like structure I began to look for a dental chair with overhead lights and the usual dental equipment. However, this place did not look like any dentist office I had ever seen in the states. It was a small room with a chair in the middle.

The dentist told me to sit down and let him take a look at my tooth. Very quickly I was told I had two options. First, to live with the pain; second, to have the tooth pulled. He was not able to do a root canal or save the tooth. Being a 20-year-old and not knowing that pulling a tooth should be the last resort, I was uncertain as to what to do. Since the pain was excruciating we decided to pull it. Then the unexpected happened. He told me they were out of Novocain and could not numb my gums. All he had was a topical numbing solution. The dentist advised me that the tooth would be pulled quickly, and I would feel only one sharp pain.

Well, he started to pull the tooth. After a few minutes of unexplainable pain I was told it was almost out. Only one final jerk was all he had to do. He told me to get ready, and at the count of three he would pull it out. Just writing about it is making me nervous. Then the dentist said one, two, and three. It felt like he pulled one of my eyes out my head. This was by far the most pain I had ever experienced. The pain went through my head, neck, eyes, and shoulders. Well at least it was over. After a week the swelling and infection cleared up.

For 20 years I did not want anyone to work on my teeth. The Veterans Administration refused to pay to have the tooth replaced after I got out of the Army. After seeing what so many combat soldiers went through, I never mentioned my dental issue to anyone for the remainder of my service.

Let's look at another one of my unexpected events. One night in our hooch, one of the men brought in a huge python snake. Supposedly, no one knew where it came from. It must have been 8 to 9 feet long. The guy holding the snake said it was harmless. That brings up two thoughts I have about the word "harmless." First, a person who has been attacked by someone's harmless pitbull might disagree with the word "harmless." Second, this reminds me of what a person says after his dog bites someone, "He has never done that before." I did not want to be the first person that this huge snake ever attacked.

Some of the men wanted to hold the snake or at least discover what it felt like. I was not one of those men. The guy with the python noticed a man who had fallen asleep on his bunk. You may have already guessed what was about to happen. They put the python on the body of this poor, unfortunate sound-asleep G.I. After the head of the snake was placed in front of his face, they woke the guy up. As his eyes opened, he saw that python. His scream was heard halfway across our compound. A fight broke out between those who thought it was funny and those who did not. One of the men took a swing at me because I was against this ridiculous prank. Truly this was an unexpected event, especially being caught up in the middle of the fight with my army cohorts.

Another unexpected event took place that could've cost me my life. Most days, some of us would get a couple hours off, referred to as "free time." We could play cards, read, or take a snooze. With one of my free times I decided to go into the city of Bien Hoa with a couple of the men. We wanted to see how the Vietnamese lived and maybe shop for a little something for our families back home. Okay, maybe to have a beer. It sounded like a good idea at the time.

After walking down a few streets and looking for something to purchase from the shops, I discovered I had lost contact with the other men. It was late afternoon and I thought of just hitching a ride back to the 90th. Soon a truck with a bunch of South Vietnamese soldiers drove by, so I jumped on their vehicle. About 10 minutes into my ride I noticed we were heading out into the country. We were not going in the direction of the 90th. I started yelling at the driver to let me off. No one could speak English, but they could see that I wanted to get off the truck. We were about five or six miles outside of the city. As I jumped out, it was obvious I was lost. The truck filled with friendly troops just went off down the road. They knew I was lost, but they seemed not to care. Now the sun was starting to set.

As I looked around all I could see were trees and fields of tall grass. The main highway was not in sight. What was I going to do? Where was I? Then I thought, *Maybe I should pray and ask God for help.* My standard prayer was, "God if you get me out of this, I promise that I will go to church." About that time a small Jeep with U.S. Army men saw me and stopped. They told me about 100 Vietcong were sighted about a mile away, headed in this direction. One of the men asked me why I was there. He said, "You could have been killed tonight." They took me all the way back to the 90th. By this time it was dark. Regretfully, I forgot to thank the Lord for answering my prayer.

That reminds me of the guy who asked the Lord for a parking space in New York City. He drove around for about an hour. Then he found one. Quickly he said, "Forget it, Lord. I just found one."

The unexpected may come at us in different ways. Sometimes it is an emotional assault. The emotional attack of loneliness tried to haunt me every day.

During my year in country (another way of saying "in Vietnam") our military had built up to just under 500,000 troops. Everywhere you went our military was present. Thousands of vehicles traveled over the roads of Vietnam. The 90th Replacement Battalion compound had over 2000 new recruits daily. Every night I slept in a hooch with about 30 men. Even with all of these people around me, I was experiencing the feeling of being alone. Oh, how I wish I would've had a personal relationship with the Lord. When we know the Son of God, we will never be alone. Psalm 46:1 reads, "God is our refuge and strength, always ready to help in times of trouble." (NLT) Other Bible translations read, "an ever-present help." When we seek the Lord we can receive that promise today. When we experience the unexpected, or when we are feeling alone or rejected, our God is a very present help.

Something that came as a complete surprise to me was the number of times a fight would break out between two of our men. The pressure we were under would come to a boiling point. Men who were trained to protect each other would start fighting. One night, such an unexpected event happened to me. As it grew time to hit the sack, some of the men in our hooch had been drinking a little too much and some were smoking pot. Fortunately, I never participated with those who used drugs. My thought was that it might be smarter to keep a clear mind and stay sharp.

A guy from Texas, a.k.a. "Tex," told a big guy from Connecticut that little David Friend from Arizona could kick his behind. How did I get into this? Admittedly I had a beer or two, but I was not drunk. The guy from Connecticut was given the nickname of "Yankee." Now Tex was insulting Yankee and saying he was afraid of David from Arizona. Here is where the unexpected took place. Yankee grabbed his knife and ran towards me. Fortunately, I was lying on my back and still had on my boots. As Yankee tried to jump on me with that knife, I rolled back, putting my boots into his chest and knocking the wind out of him. Since I was not a fighter, I was the most surprised guy in that hooch. Now don't misunderstand me. I am not saying I am a tough guy, but I discovered that proper training had prepared me for the unexpected. That applies to life in general.

Vietnam was filled with constant unexpected events. When you think about it, life is filled with the unexpected. We must prepare ourselves for such events. We can do that as we rely upon the Word of God.

Still another event hit me by surprise in Vietnam. One day while on perimeter guard duty, I felt a pain in my lower back. The pain started in my groin and moved around to where my kidney was located. That pain was not new to me. From the age of 16, I had experienced kidney stones. This was another kidney stone. My thoughts went back to the physical I had at the induction center before being sworn into the Army. The doctor had asked me about my kidneys. Because I did not want to look like a guy who was trying to find a way out of serving his country, I did not tell the doctor the whole truth about my history with kidney issues.

During the examination I told the doctor my kidneys were just fine. The truth was, I had experienced kidney problems as a teenager. Passing stones and having bladder and kidney infections were common to me. So there I was on the perimeter alone with a kidney stone. The pain was intense. My replacement was not due for another hour. Once again I looked to the heavens to pray to the God Who I had not accepted. "God, please take this pain away." It seemed like an eternity before I was rescued by the next guy scheduled to guard my post.

Quickly, I ran back to see a nurse. They took me to the 93rd evacuation hospital in Long Binh. As I was rushed to the emergency area, it seemed like a dozen nurses and doctors came to my rescue. I felt a little embarrassed to be in a hospital in Vietnam with only a kidney stone. The medical crew was amazing. They did everything they could to comfort me.

This was an unexpected event for me that night. Yet, an even greater unexpected event was about to take place. As I laid on my bed still feeling the pain, the doors of the emergency room flew open and about a dozen victims of an ambush were brought in and laid next to me. The men had every type of wound you could imagine. Some with leg, head, or arm injuries. Several men had been hit with shrapnel in numerous places on their bodies. As I tried to sit up, I saw a man walking in with a hole going through his body. You could see light on the other side of his body. Never had I seen such a horrible example of war.

Now I understood why I was there in that hospital. Here I was complaining to God about a kidney stone, while some of these men were facing a death sentence. For the first time since coming to Vietnam, I saw up close the results of man's inhumanity to man. Without exception, the men who were wounded were shouting they were okay, just help someone else. Since that night, I have gained a greater respect for those who have been wounded in war and for those who care for their injuries.

Today, some of the men I know who served in Vietnam have received a Purple Heart for an injury they sustained in action. May God bless these men. May the Lord protect all those who are in war-torn countries. Our country must always help those who have come back wounded or with diseases and emotional scars.

I will never forget the unexpected event I witnessed at the 93rd evacuation hospital. That night prepared me for future events in my life. We must expect the unexpected in life. My prayer is we will be prepared through our faith in a God Who promised to never leave us or forsake us. We must believe He is a very present help in times of facing the unexpected.

A person who is trained in the Word of God is prepared for the unexpected. This might be a good time to look into God's Word and get ready for whatever may try to attack us in life. Ephesians 6:10-11 reads,

> "A final word: Be strong in the Lord and in his mighty power. Put on all of God's armor so that you will be able to stand firm against all strategies of the devil." (NLT)

The Scripture goes on to tell us to use God's Word to fight our battles. We are to be truthful and righteous in our thinking. We are to be at peace and have faith in God to protect us. Then we must pray for God's wisdom to help us through the unexpected events we will face.

LIFE APPLICATION

Life is filled with unexpected events. They can be serious like a car accident, a disease, loss of a job, or even a pregnancy. Fortunately, most of the unexpected things we experience are minor. These can include a friend not returning your call, stubbing your toe, burning your dinner, spilling something on your favorite shirt, and running out of gas in your car. It is not the unexpected event that is important. What is crucial, is how we deal with the unexpected. Being prepared is the answer to facing anything unexpected. We must believe whatever we will face in life has a purpose to strengthen who we are. Expect the unexpected, and we will be able to deal with anything.

Near one of the perimeter guard stations on the 90th. Most of my duty was at night.

Sharon sent me this picture so I could see how she was growing with our baby boy. She did not want to send me one but eventually she gave in. I was so happy she did.

A river in the Mekong Delta where someone was fishing for dinner. They were never happy about us disturbing the waters and running the fish away.

"Older men declare war. But it is the youth that must fight and die."

HERBERT HOOVER

Tet Offensive

January 21, 1968 was my wife Sharon's 21st birthday. Because of that, we planned to meet around the 21st of January in Hawaii. Once a year, Vietnam soldiers were given a five- to seven-day rest and recuperation leave, a.k.a. "R&R." The common places to take R&R were Bangkok, Thailand, Japan, Australia, Hawaii, Taiwan, and Singapore. Shortly after our son was born, I put in for my R&R to Hawaii. It was approved for January 23rd to January 30, 1968. Sharon was in Phoenix and planned to meet me in Hawaii. She was able to get a friend to care for our three-month old son Eddie. We met and had an amazing week in Paradise.

R&R was like heaven to those of us who were able to go. Sharon and I drove around Oahu to see God's creation. We went out to see the USS Arizona in Pearl Harbor. It was the first ship to go down when the Japanese attacked Pearl Harbor, December 7th, 1941. Visiting the site where over 2400 men lost their life was a very sobering experience. However, after being in Vietnam and seeing body bags lying on the tarmac of the Tan Son Nhut Airbase, I better understood how death was a part of war.

We were a little concerned about how the people of Hawaii would treat a Vietnam veteran. During our R&R, we were blessed to discover almost every place we ate gave us a 50% reduction on our bill. Everywhere in Hawaii the people were very kind to us. As our week came to an end, we went to church at the top of a high-rise building in Waikiki. We had not given our hearts to the Lord, but we did have an opportunity to pray and give God thanks for our time together. The time we had alone was wonderful. Intimacy in marriage is God's plan.

To the married men reading this, I need to share a little pastoral advice. The most intimate thing you can do with your wife is to pray with her. That is probably the best marital advice you will ever receive. Prayer with your wife shows reliance on God. Prayer requires transparency between married couples.

When I left to go back to Vietnam and Sharon went back to Phoenix we were sad, yet received comfort, that in less than two months I would return home. Soon we would get to be together for a lifetime.

We had no way of knowing what was about to happen in Vietnam. Allow me to give you an explanation of what I was about to fly into.

Early in the morning of January 30, 1968, (this was the time I was heading back to Vietnam) the North Vietnamese Army, a.k.a. "NVA," and the Vietcong put together a countrywide assault on 13 cities, towns, and military installations in South Vietnam. This was called the Tet offensive. It was the Vietnamese New Year. Although the assault would be turned back by American and Allied troops, thousands of military and civilians would die. The Tet offensive was said to have continued until the fall of 1968. Approximately 58,000 of the NVA and Vietcong were killed during Tet. The intensity of fighting from the 80,000 NVA and Vietcong attack surprised South Vietnamese and American soldiers. The Tet took the lives of nearly 4,000 Americans. The South Vietnamese had nearly 5,000 killed in that action. The Tet offensive took place during the Tet holiday truce. Even the US Embassy in Saigon was attacked by a suicide squad of 19 men. These men temporarily took control of the grounds around the embassy compound. They were called a suicide squad because all 19 were trapped and killed inside the compound.

Most believe the Tet offensive turned the direction of the Vietnam War. America made a major shift in its plans. Instead of believing we would defeat the Communists, we now wanted to find a way to pull out and train the South Vietnamese to fight their own war. The Tet offensive was the first step toward the end of President Johnson's presidency.

The television coverage of the Tet caused American citizens to see the severity of this war. Tet brought forth an increase of war protests in America. Some of the protesters even turned against American troops. Names like "baby killers," "rapists," and "murderers" deeply impacted our troops who served in Vietnam when they returned home to America. Many of our veterans still carry the emotional scars of being rejected by their country.

I was due back from my R&R at the 90th on January 30, 1968. January 30th was the beginning of the TET offensive. As Sharon was flying back to Phoenix, I was in the air heading toward Vietnam as the Tet offensive erupted. My plane approached Tan Son Nhut airbase and the pilot announced we would make a very quick stop. He told us the airport was under attack from the North Vietnamese Army and an offensive front had broken out over the entire country. Since this was a commercial airline we had stopped in Guam to drop off most of the passengers. Only eight to ten of us were going to Vietnam.

As we flew into Tan Son Nhut, I could see mortars and machine gun fire near the airport. My first thought was, *Sharon does not know about this.* Then I thought, *Why don't we just turn this plane around and fly back to Hawaii.* The wheels of the plane touched down. The airport began to receive incoming small arms fire and mortar rounds. We could see a truck with stairs attached and a platform mounted on it driving out to meet us. We stood at the doorway as the plane stopped. When the door opened everyone was shouting at us to get out, get out, get out. We jumped on the truck's landing and stairs. Then the truck started to drive away. Instantly, the airplane turned around and flew off faster than it had landed. The truck driver drove us across the tarmac to the terminal. Chaos was everywhere. Sand-bagged bunkers were being built around the airport. Helicopters were flying in every direction.

Now what do I do? Trying to pray, I felt a loss for words. How can I get back to the 90th Replacement Battalion? Inside the terminal, I asked if there were any trucks going to the 90th. That was a silly question under these circumstances. I might as well have asked for a super shuttle or Taxi. All I knew was I had to find a ride on Highway One from Saigon. We were told to stay off the streets of Saigon. The entire city was under attack.

Still in civilian clothes and without a weapon, I had to get back to the 90th or I thought I would be charged with being absent without leave, a.k.a. "AWOL." On the main road there were US and South Vietnamese vehicles going in every direction. Fortunately, I hopped a ride down Highway One towards the 90th. Along the way we experienced enemy small arms weapons firing wildly in every direction on that roadway. About 100 yards from the main gate of the 90th they had to drop me off because they were heading in another direction. Again the hand of the Lord had directed my path. The God I had rejected had protected me.

As I approached the gate an order was yelled at me to stop and identify myself. After shouting to them who I was, they asked me for the code word for today. Well, I had just flown in from R&R in Hawaii with my bride. How could I know today's code word? After a few minutes of screaming at each other, the security sergeant ordered me to walk slowly with my hands raised high. It was still dark and difficult for those at the gate to recognize me. That's when I wished I was six feet six and 250 pounds, so I could be seen. However I was about the same size of the Vietcong at five foot six, 140 pounds, with dark hair. It's no wonder they were cautious with me.

As I approached the gate the sergeant in charge recognized me. He told me to get my rifle and gear together and run to my regular guard bunker to be ready for a possible Vietcong assault on our compound. That was a lot to process, especially since only a few hours earlier I had been with my wife on a beach in Hawaii.

During the Tet offensive the Vietcong and North Vietnamese Army believed the South Vietnamese Army and civilians would rise up against America and its allies. Thankfully, this never happened. The Vietcong and NVA had to fight with their original attack force.

Quickly, I joined the other cadre at the 90th on the perimeter. Most were clerks, cooks, and administrative guys. We were responsible for approximately 2,000 unarmed men on our compound. What if the Vietcong or NVA would overrun our perimeter? How many casualties would we have? From our compound we could see flames around the city of Bien Hoa. The ammunition dump in Long Binh was on fire. At first we saw a great wall of fire, then an orange cloud in the form of a mushroom. The force of the explosion blew off some of the overhanging window cutouts on our buildings. I am not sure of the distance between that explosion and our quarters.

As we awaited a possible assault from the Vietcong, we heard an incredible sound as if from heaven. Several cobra assault helicopters began to fire rockets in front of our perimeter. From somewhere, machine gun fire combed the area. The explosions revealed a number of enemy hiding in the foliage just outside our compound. We were ordered to fire upon that area. Then all of a sudden everything became quiet. Today, I thank the Lord for those cobra helicopters and His hand of protection. Then I wondered what Sharon knew about Tet.

The next few days we were expecting another offensive attack. At night we could see tracer rounds and an occasional mortar explosion close to our compound. In a couple of days, we went back to our old system of security. Almost every night we would still go out alone to our perimeter guard bunkers. Thankfully, I had only a few weeks before going home. To our surprise, the civilians were back to their routines within a few days. We would see young girls walk up to the main gate trying to sell souvenirs, candy, beer, and cokes to our men. It's sad to say, the Vietnamese civilians had become accustomed to war. It became their way of life.

Even though our compound was under attack during Tet, the Lord blessed me with a great assignment in Vietnam. As I mentioned before, sometimes I would feel a little guilty about my assignment. Especially when we had assigned thousands of men into some of the worst fighting in South Vietnam. Except for being alone on nightly perimeter guard duty and occasional patrols in the surrounding areas, the 90th was one of the best places I could've served. That was just another example of God's hand being upon my life.

When the Tet offensive hit, everything changed in Vietnam. We knew from that night forward we would not win the war. Even the faith of our men changed. Prior to Tet, some of the men at the 90th said they were atheists and did not believe in any type of God. However, during the nights of Tet almost everyone was praying.

While the Tet was raging all over South Vietnam, I wondered if the people in America knew what was happening. How was my wife Sharon doing? Remember, she flew back to Phoenix from our R&R rendezvous in Hawaii the same time I flew to Vietnam. The next day she heard about the Tet Offensive. We were not able to talk to each other. Cell phones or Skyping were not in existence. During my time in Vietnam I had written to my beautiful wife every day. She did the same to me. When Tet hit, the letters stopped coming. It took almost two weeks before we received any mail. Sharon decided not to look at the news on television or in the newspaper. People would ask her about how I was doing. Then they would want to go into detail about the number killed or wounded during Tet. Sharon would always stop them and say, "David will be just fine."

My wife is an amazing woman. During Tet, she focused her attention on loving our son. She lived alone in a guest house. She would work part-time jobs where she could keep our son with her. It was hard for me to imagine how she must have felt during the Tet Offensive. Even though she had not become a follower of Jesus Christ, she knew if she prayed God would hear and answer her prayers. May her faith be a source of strength to any woman who has or may face a difficult trial.

As soon as I started this book, I asked my wife to write about her experiences at home during the Tet Offensive. Following are Sharon's comments concerning that difficult time in her life:

At the time my husband David was in Vietnam, I was renting a guesthouse from an older couple. They were very kind and concerned for me and our infant son. Knowing where my husband was stationed, the mailman, who at that time delivered door-to-door, personally made sure I was in receipt of all my mail.

I had a map of Vietnam and years earlier in school had done a report on Laos; therefore, I felt a little familiar with where David was located.

I purposely stayed away from the newspapers. For one thing, I could not afford a subscription, and the other, I knew the worry would be very difficult to handle. I was a 21-year-old married woman with a baby and it was hard to understand how I could be without this wonderful guy I loved. I knew first and foremost he would be the best he could be in serving our country, and I was very proud of him, but I missed him so terribly from morning to night. My sweetest God-given gift for both of us was our son. I took great comfort in having our son with me every day.

David wrote every day and his letters were always delivered very timely. We also had tape recorders so we could hear each other's voices. There were no cell phones; what we would have given to be able to talk to each other.

R&R in Hawaii was like a dream to us. The people were so pleasant and respectful and we had reduced prices at restaurants. I flew back to Phoenix and gathered up our son who I had left with a friend. I was so excited to think in just a few months David would be home.

However, a friend gave me a newspaper the following day. I was shocked to see the news of the Tet offensive. I knew David had flown into Vietnam when the Tet had erupted. Going directly home, I scanned every detail given in the paper and went to the map which showed where the Vietcong were going through the villages and of course into Saigon and the Bien Hoa area.

Crying and praying were not unfamiliar to me through these months, but this was the most strenuous time of all. The over two weeks in which I did not receive any mail from him was unusual. I tried to have control over my thought life, believing he was safe, even though I knew he was in the midst of fighting in a war I did not understand.

I ran to the mailbox every day and the mailman gave me the most compassionate looks. It's interesting to think sometimes we just don't know what to say to each other in times like this. Even parents and family and friends are silent, but the warmth of their hugs and love in their eyes say what we need to hear.

The pastor at the church I was attending prayed for our military men every week and knew of this movement in Vietnam. It seemed his prayers were far more intense.

Then that special letter came to say he was okay. Though I did not have a close relationship with the Lord then, I knew enough to be thankful.

When David returned home, we did not talk a lot about Vietnam. For many months he would wake up as if he were there, sweat pouring down over him, sitting up in bed as if he had his rifle in hand. I would be still, sometimes moving off of the bed onto the floor, just waiting for this time to pass, and little by little, it did. He would always say it felt so real, like he was there again.

We moved to Fort Ord, California to finish his time in the Army. I was told there was going to be an award given to him on the parade grounds at Fort Ord. I really didn't know what this was all about, but dressed nicely and took Edward, our infant son with us. When they took me to where I was to sit, it was with Army officers and wives on a high, large platform. There were hundreds of uniformed men on the field in formation. I was astounded at the way they honored David as he was given the Army commendation medal. As the uniformed men marched by saluting, I realized this was a sign to these men, "Yes you can come home to those waiting for you. Many will not come home but this is to give you hope for the future."

Thank you Sharon for your words. It's a little hard for me to read and keep it together.

After leaving Vietnam I put everything I had into forgetting that terrible place. Often, I would be asked questions about my experiences there. The first question was usually if I had killed anyone in Vietnam. Young men or women should never have to experience war. They should also never have to come back to a country that treated them so poorly. It has been over 50 years since I came home from Vietnam. For 30 to 40 years I kept silent about my service there. My prayer is that in some way this book will be able to help Vietnam veterans and their families. Now that I am a follower of Jesus Christ, I can see how His hand has always been on me. Never forget that whatever you go through, our God is always a prayer away. He loves you and has a plan for your life. Seek Him and you will always find His love.

Sometimes my experiences in Vietnam challenge my memory. Because of that, I have re-examined those experiences. After researching the events of Tet at the 90th I feel confident my words are the true events I encountered. In no way am I trying to glorify my involvement in Vietnam. My prayer is if there is any glory to be given, it must go to my Lord and Savior Jesus

Christ. To Him be all glory and praise for all the things He has done.

LIFE APPLICATION

America has sent many into war to defend our country. Those who faced the trials of war may continue to experience emotional and physical challenges. Whatever we face in life may challenge our faith and trust in a higher power. We must never forget that our God is a very present help in the trials of life. Put your trust in Him and He will never forsake you.

We were blessed to meet in Hawaii for my R&R from Vietnam. We had no idea that I would fly back into the Tet Offensive.

Sharon and our son Ed in Phoenix while I was going through the Tet Offensive. Ed was her source of Joy.

Fort Ord graduation parade where I was blessed with the Army Commendation Medal for my Vietnam Service. Maybe they wanted to show the new guys that even a little guy could make it back from Vietnam.

That's me in the middle. I asked them if I could pass on the parade. You guessed it, I was seriously requested to attend. Sharon sat with Eddie on the platform.

"It's not over until it's over but it's almost."

JOHN BREAUX, U.S. SENATOR

CHAPTER 11

Short Timer

Almost immediately after I arrived in Vietnam I started to count down the number of days until I returned home. Everyone I knew had what was called a "short timer's calendar." My calendar was by my bunk. Each day, I would put an "X" over the previous day. Because of certain military actions, we were not able to keep the calendar up-to-date at times. But then it was always great to be able to mark off several days all at once. Seeing an entire month crossed out with X's was great.

However, looking back on that process I don't think it was a very good idea. It was depressing in my early months in country. We were focused too often on how long we had to go before going home. Maybe only the last month would have been a better short timer's calendar.

In Ephesians 5:16 the apostle Paul gave us some good advice on how to deal with our days. *"Make the most of every opportunity in these evil days."* (NLT) His advice was to make the best out of every day and try to find some joy in it.

We can live a life that is more enjoyable every day. Today, I am focused on getting the most out of each day. My favorite day of the week has always been Monday. I realize most of the people we know dread Monday. This reminds me of a cartoon

I would see in the lunchroom when I worked at a bank. The first box was labeled Monday and the guy was sad and slumped over. The next box was labeled Tuesday.

The same character was still sad and looked forlorn. Wednesday was the third box. This time the character had a little grin and walked up straight. The Thursday box showed a guy with a smile and a positive step. But on Friday he was jumping and laughing. The final box had a sign that read, "Thank God it's Friday." That silly cartoon is how many feel about their work week. The reason I have always liked Mondays is because it sets the stage for everything we can accomplish that week. Monday is the foundation we build the rest of the week on. This may sound strange to some of you, but Mondays made the rest of the week enjoyable to me.

The short timer's calendar is very similar to that cartoon. It made you feel down for many months. Being in Vietnam was bad enough, and that calendar made it a little more miserable.

How do you look at your work week? Is Monday a bummer? Do you live from weekend to weekend? Growing up, my Mom and Dad did not enjoy their work weeks. They were great parents and always provided for our needs. However, I always wondered why they did not work in something they wanted to do.

My Grandmother was different when it came to work. She always seemed to look forward to going to work. She was an entrepreneur. She owned a small motel and several restaurants during the years we lived near her. Grandmother worked very hard, usually 6-7 days a week. But, I never remember her talking about the weekend being something to look forward to. Besides, she always worked on the weekends and she enjoyed her work. My Grandmother would talk to me about why hard work was so rewarding. She told me to never work in something you do not enjoy. My Grandmother would not have liked the short timer's calendar I had. She would have told me to try and find something good in every day.

As my tour was coming to an end, I was called into headquarters to meet with the personnel director of the 90th. The director asked me how I was doing. My response was something like, "Only 30 days to go Sargent." This was around the middle of February 1968, only about 15 days after the Tet Offensive.

Without showing any emotion, the sergeant told me he had an offer for me. He stated that my two-year commitment to the Army would be up on October 18, 1968. That meant I still had seven months of active duty after I finished my tour in Vietnam. Before I could think about where he was going with all of this, he quickly explained to me if I would extend my stay in Vietnam I could get out of the Army July 18, 1968. Then he said the Army would give me a $5,000 bonus to stay in Vietnam until July 18, 1968. At the time I was making about $150 a month. That bonus would be equal to nearly 3 years of my current pay.

My head went down and I asked if this was voluntary. Now, don't forget I had already been taken advantage of when the recruiter said volunteering for the draft would give me a good assignment. The words "volunteering" and "Army" were not a good combination to me.

Then Sarge advised me this would be my choice. He would not put any pressure on me to stay in Vietnam, or to go back to the states. Looking him directly in the eyes I asked him, "If I go home, where will I be assigned? Will my wife and son be allowed to be with me?" He responded immediately to my questions, "You will be assigned to Fort Ord, California for the remainder of your commitment. Yes, your family can be with you."

I remember my response as if it was yesterday. "Let me get this straight. It's either four more months here, with the possibility of an extension of the Tet Offensive, or seven more months with my beautiful, sexy wife and our son Eddie." He knew what was coming. With a smile I said, "With all due respect the answer is no."

Then he said something that surprised me. "That is a good decision son." That's when I gave him one of my reasons for being opposed to extending my time in Vietnam. In April 1967, a good friend of mine had been killed in combat near the DMZ. We attended school together from first grade through high school. He was a Marine. He was offered a package to extend and he took it. Shortly thereafter, his life was taken from him in combat. His name was Ed. He left behind a pretty girl and his family I knew from South Mountain High School. We named our son after this brave hero.

After this meeting, I felt a great weight of stress and anxiety lift from my shoulders. With only about 30 days to go, I became extremely careful about every move I made. The company commander of the 90th gave the order that all cadre with 30 days or less to spend in country, would not be required to go on any patrols. However, perimeter guard duty would still be required until returning to the United States. It was not until I had 30 days remaining in Vietnam that I believed I would make it back home alive and with all my limbs.

Those who served in combat areas like Vietnam, and more recently the Middle East, are usually very young. They are in the early years of their life. Yet most wondered daily if they would survive. Sadly, many of our veterans return home severely wounded or missing limbs. Some are facing physical and mental challenges. It is a terrible state of affairs when injured veterans have to almost beg for help. Our country must never forget the sacrifices that have been made by those who have worn the uniforms of the U.S. military. We must apply pressure on Congress to provide for the needs of American Veterans.

Having a short-timer's attitude in a combat area may be okay. In life, however, we must enjoy every day in order live out God's purpose for us. Living life from weekend to weekend is destructive. Living every day with an expectation that something good is about to happen will bring life. The words of Jesus about how to live each day are found in John 10:10, *"The thief's purpose is to steal and kill and destroy. My purpose is to give them a rich and satisfying life."* (NLT)

The word "thief" refers to the devil. The words "rich and satisfying life" are sometimes translated, "have life and have it abundantly."

If you are living like that person with a weekend to weekend affliction of "Thank God it's Friday," you can change that thinking to "Thank God it's Today." Let's focus on Psalms 118:24, *"This is the day that the Lord has made. We will rejoice and be glad in it."* (NLT)

LIFE APPLICATION

When we spend all of our time thinking, "I can't wait until something in the future will happen," we will miss out on what may happen today. My Pastor for 20 years always said that he lived each day for what was in it. He referred to each day as a wet washcloth. He wound squeeze every drop out of it. We need to enjoy each day as a new opportunity. Living for the weekend robs us of each day's potential.

"The thoughts of coming home have never changed. Experiencing it is nothing but joy."

AUTHOR UNKNOWN

SECTION III
After Vietnam

DAVID C. FRIEND

CHAPTER 12

Coming Home

Finally it was March 18, 1968. We have all seen the pictures of veterans coming home to America and getting down on their knees and kissing the ground. I have always thought that was kind of corny. Why would anyone want to embarrass themselves with that silly gesture? Well you guessed it, as soon as I walked down the steps of the plane that brought me home to America, I got down and kissed the ground. As I looked around, a number of other men did the same thing. It was great to be back in the USA. The thoughts of being with my wife, Sharon, and our son, Eddie, were overwhelming. Seeing the rest of my family would be great. Driving my own car to Bob's Big Boy hamburgers with my family would become a reality.

After arriving at Travis Air Force Base in northern California, I was told to report for duty at Fort Ord, California in three weeks. A Greyhound bus was parked off the base with a sign that read, "San Francisco airport." About 25 to 30 guys all loaded into that bus to get their lives in America reignited again. The drive was about an hour and half from Travis Air Force Base to the San Francisco airport. As we pulled onto the highway, my mind started to fill up with questions. Being a fairly organized guy and always planning for the future, I made a list of everything I thought we needed to get accomplished.

1. Where can Sharon and I live near Fort Ord?
2. Will our car be okay to drive there from Phoenix?
3. How much will it cost to live in Monterey, California?
4. Where will I work when I get out of the Army?
5. Those 1968 Chevy Camaros look good – I want one.
6. What kind of work will I do at Fort Ord?
7. Sharon may have to work, who will watch Eddie?
8. Can the Army call me back to Vietnam?
9. How will civilians in the US treat me?
10. We need to find a church.

Those of us who were coming back into the United States had lists of things to accomplish. Soon the bus drove us to the front of the airport, but we were told we would not be allowed to get off. The driver told us there was a Vietnam War protest going on at the terminal. It was filled with draft dodgers, flower children, and potheads. In the distance we could see signs that said, "Welcome baby killers. Stop the war. Why did you go?"

One of the guys yelled out, "Can we get out of the bus and just talk to these folks?" Another guy said, "Yeah I talk with my fist." Then all of us wanted to get out of the bus and have a face-to-face confrontation with these protesters. That's when a police officer stepped in our bus and told us he wanted to do a little talking to the protesters, as he lifted his nightstick. I know we were biased in our attitude toward the protestors, and it was their right to protest. But we were not "rapists" and "baby killers." However, we were pretty good at convincing others to see our point of view. After all, we went to fight so they could have freedom to protest. They did not know what we had gone through and neither did it seem they cared.

The doors of our bus closed and we drove to another area of the terminal where we would not have contact with anyone.

I started to think of the welcome the men received when they came home from World War II. A strong feeling of confusion, mixed with rejection, came over me. How would the rest of America treat us?

The airlines were very kind to us as we were taken to the front of the lines and given early boarding on our plane. Only three or four of us flew to Phoenix. The other men went back to their area of our great country. All of us had to think about what kind of reception we would get back home.

After I landed in Phoenix, I walked down the stairs of our aircraft toward the terminal. As I walked across the tarmac it was a radical change from the tarmac in Tan Son Nhut air force base in Vietnam, with its body bags being shipped back to America. In 1968, Sky Harbor Airport was about one-tenth the size of what it is today. We did not have the long interior walkways.

As I entered the gate, there stood my brown-eyed girl crying tears of joy. She had Eddie in her arms. Just like the thousands who were coming home daily, we had our little family reunion among hundreds of strangers at the airport. As we walked through the terminal we received an amazing welcome. I can remember holding Eddie high over my head. People were clapping, smiling, and shouting, "Welcome home," some holding their hands over their hearts. Although the terminal was small, the walkway seemed like a mile long to me. There were no protesters and no hateful signs, only people happy to see a family being reunited.

We drove back to the guest house in the backyard of the lady's home where Sharon had been living the past year. My family understood we needed to be alone together that day.

After a week of visiting with family and friends, we had to pack up and head to Fort Ord. Everything we owned was loaded into the trunk and backseat of our 1961 Buick Skylark. Eddie's mattress fit great on top of the stuff packed in the backseat. We thought he could play and sleep while we drove to California. Today, we would probably get arrested because of the way we packed up that car. No seatbelts or child restraints were required back then.

About halfway to Fort Ord our car overheated. The mechanic said we needed a new radiator. The repair was about $100. That was equal to what I was paid by the Army each month. Thankfully Sharon and I were able to save $1,000 from my military pay plus the money I made working part-time at the NCO and officers bar at the 90th. Yes, you read that correctly. I was a bartender for a few hours at night before I went out to my perimeter guard duty post. All of the money I made was sent home to Sharon so we could save up for our move to my next assignment. Although I do not drink, I can remember how to make most types of mixed drinks. Sometimes when we watch the television show Jeopardy they will have a category on mixed drinks. Usually I get most of those Jeopardy questions correct.

We arrived at Fort Ord and were given a day to find a place to live in the Monterey, California area. Our first place was a room in the back of a large home. That is all we could afford. After living there for about a month, we decided having our bed, Eddie's crib, and all of our stuff in a 15 by 20 foot room would not work for us. So we found a little 600 square foot house in Seaside, California. It was next to Fort Ord. The rent was $60 a month and it was fully furnished. After a few months we discovered some of the furniture was full of sand fleas. That made the sofa and chair off-limits. My mom and dad came to visit us about a month after we got our little house. I sprayed our furniture to get rid of the sand fleas. Mom and Dad slept on the sofa bed in the living room and did not tell us until years later that the sand fleas kept them up all night.

Our time in Northern California was great. Sharon found a job she loved at the Bank of America in Seaside. Even though we only had seven months left on my two-year Army commitment they were willing to hire her. We had the weekends off and would occasionally drive up to San Francisco on a Saturday to do some sightseeing. In 1968 there were a lot of sites to see in San Francisco, many of them were the people.

We would drive through the Haight Asberry section and watch the flower children dance and sing in the streets. They were smoking pot as they danced and blocked the traffic. It reminded me of all the men I witnessed using pot while I served in Vietnam.

Although I never smoked a joint, I admit to drinking a lot of low-alcohol content beer. If you would have seen the green, sometimes yellowish, water we were supposed to drink you would've chosen the beer also. As soon as I returned from Vietnam I stopped drinking almost any type of alcohol. My family was so important to me I did not want anything to come between us. Many of the Vietnam veterans came back with drug or alcohol addictions. Very little help has been given to most of them. Even though I was not a Christian, I thank the Lord for helping me stay away from those influences.

During my time at Fort Ord we lived near Monterey, California. The Monterey Pop Festival started near us in 1967. In the summer of 1968 we would drive or walk by the festival to see who was performing. One night we decided to walk outside the gates and listen to the music. We could not afford to buy a ticket to go inside. That night we heard Janis Joplin, Jimi Hendrix, and the Who (a famous group). These were some of the biggest rock stars in the world. Looking back, it is sad to think of the number of rock groups that promoted drugs with their music. Janis Joplin, Jimi Hendrix, and members of the Who all died of drug overdoses. The Vietnam War and the decade of the 60s brought a drug culture to America that has continued to devastate our country to this day.

Vietnam was known as the "unpopular" war. It is hard to imagine how any war could be popular unless they attacked our borders. America treated the World War II soldiers as heroes, and they most certainly were. The Korean veterans had the support of most Americans. However, the Vietnam War veterans were treated with hatred and rejection. The Vietnam War became the most divisive war since the Civil War.

After and during the war, our government sent 2,700,000 Vietnam veterans back to their families. Some of those veterans would continue a career in the military. However, all Vietnam veterans had to face the same ridicule and resentment. Most of these returning veterans received little or no assistance with their adjustment back to civilian life. In my case, I was given a one-day readjustment training session. The session was with a group of vets and lasted only a few hours. No wonder so many Vietnam veterans have struggled for so many decades.

Hundreds of thousands of families were trying to be re-united after their experiences with Vietnam. Often I have wondered how many of these marriages survived the impact of that war. Where would the returning veterans get good jobs? How were the veterans treated upon returning home? The Vietnam veterans spent 12 to 13 months in a combat zone. How would they adjust? Those veterans with whom I have spoken to say they received less than one day of counseling towards making the transition. Today we have about 40,000 homeless veterans in America. Nearly 300,000 Vietnam Vets suffer today with physical and emotional issues they received from Vietnam.

America must care for its veterans. My personal experience has been terrible with the Phoenix Veterans hospital. When I lost my right kidney to cancer, the Veterans Administration took four years to look into my claim for help. To this day they have not correctly addressed the reason for my claim.

One of the disasters of Vietnam was the use of Agent Orange. It was used to kill vegetation, and now it is killing veterans who fought and/or worked in it. It is time our government takes full responsibility for the health care of all veterans. Congress can, and must, be in unity to provide the care our veterans of all wars require.

Most of the veterans I speak to are very reserved in their comments about their service in Vietnam. When I returned home, my plan was to never discuss my service with anyone. If I was at a dinner party with our friends or family I always kept quiet if the subject of Vietnam was brought up. Back in 1968, I was ashamed to have ever served there. My wife Sharon was so helpful in allowing me to put aside my experiences.

As I was writing this book my daughter, Tricia, said her brother, Ed, and her tried to talk to me about my service in Vietnam when they were very young. They have said I would always change the subject. As a matter of fact, both Tricia and Ed seem to be a little concerned about how I would handle digging up so much of what I had buried since 1968.

Other than my wife, the only person I have spoken to at length about my Vietnam service is my friend Pete. He served in the Marines near the DMZ. Over breakfast, we have talked about our experiences. Some of them bad, but many we even laugh about today. Thanks, Pete, for the hours of healing I received during breakfast.

Sharon mentioned in her comments in chapter 10 that when I returned from Vietnam I went through a lot of night sweats. At times, she would be concerned about how I might act in the middle of the night. We both knew those experiences would go away. Although I don't remember sitting up and talking at night, I do recall having dreams I was called back to Vietnam. Those nightmares lasted for many years. The dreams seemed so real, I would imagine Sharon and our children going out to the airport to send me away.

About four years after returning from Vietnam, Sharon and I accepted the Lord Jesus Christ as our Savior, and everything in our lives changed.

When I became a Christian the dreams went away. The Holy Spirit replaced those nightmares with dreams of a future with hope. With my desire to read God's word, I discovered a Scripture that changed my life. Jeremiah 29:11, *"I know the plans I have for you,' says the Lord. 'They are plans for good and not for disaster, to give you a future and a hope.'"* (NLT) That Scripture is God's plan for your life, too. Read it and live in it with expectation. As you are challenged with issues in life, you will be able to come home to the comfort of God's Word.

LIFE APPLICATION

It feels good to come home anytime we have been away for a long vacation or family visit. There is an old saying, "Home is where the heart is." When I served in Vietnam, all I could think about was going back home. When we raised our children, we moved a lot from home to home. Some of these moves were due to work transfers. Other moves came because of our home-building business. Our kids have said they did not have many memories due to our moving so often. We have always told them they have lots of memories; it's just hard to know where those memories were made. Going home may not be a good thought to everyone, however, going back to the good memories of life will always be good.

Back at Fort Ord to serve my last 7 months of duty. We lived in the city of Seaside.

My beautiful wife and son in Seaside. The army offered me four more months in Vietnam and I could get out of the Army early, or seven months at Fort Ord. Good choice, right?

"Wishing to be friends is quick work, but friendship is a slow ripening fruit."

ARISTOTLE

CHAPTER 13

Friends of Vietnam

As I have expressed previously, during my year in Vietnam I had a lot of acquaintances. But only one was my true friend. That may be true in your life. Sadly, I have not been able to locate my Vietnam friend. Wherever this man is today, my prayer is that he will live a long and productive life. May the Lord bless him and keep him.

Although I can remember having only one friend in Vietnam while I served there, I am happy to say I have made many Vietnam veteran friendships after I came home. It seems every week I meet someone who served in Vietnam. As soon as one Vietnam vet meets another Vietnam vet a common bond is made immediately. That is true with all veterans in all the branches of service and with all the places they have served. Oh it's true, there is a little competition between some of the military branches. My friend, Pete, who served in Vietnam was a Marine. He left there before I did. Sometimes he will grin and say that when he left Vietnam we were winning. That is ok, Pete. We both know the Army usually has to stay and clean up.

Veterans who I am proud of are my brother, Jim, who served in the Air Force in Florida for four years during the Cuban Missile Crisis. Then there is my brother-in-law, Rich, who also served in the Air Force for four years. He was in Scotland and Turkey. You can see they were smarter than me. Think about it, Florida, Scotland, or Vietnam, which one should I have chosen? Thanks, Jim and Rich, for your service.

There is an amazing man I know who served in Vietnam. He has been a major blessing in my life. His name is Dave Roever. Dave joined the Navy and served as a riverboat gunner. In his eighth months in Vietnam he was burned beyond recognition when a phosphorous grenade he was attempting to throw exploded in his hand. He was hospitalized for 14 months, where he underwent numerous major surgeries. His survival and life afterwards are miraculous. Today, Dave is the founder of an amazing ministry to wounded veterans. In addition, he has been a traveling evangelist and speaker for nearly 50 years. I will never forget the day I met Dave. He was speaking at our church, Phoenix First Assembly. After his powerful and surprisingly funny message, he invited all the Vietnam veterans to come to the front of our 5,000 seat sanctuary. At first I did not want to go up front. After all, I was not very proud of my Vietnam service. However, Dave continued to ask all of us to come forward. A still, quiet voice spoke to me and I felt something amazing would happen if I obeyed that voice in my heart to walk up front. It was the voice of the Holy Spirit telling me this was my moment. As I stood in front of Dave he told us with a voice of compassion and strength, "Welcome home." That hit me like I had run into a wall. All at once, I felt it was okay to have served in that unpopular war. Dave told us to turn to those around us and tell them welcome home.

My wife and family made me feel welcome upon my return from Vietnam. But there was something different about this man who had experienced something worse than I could ever imagine. Dave's body still shows the results of his many surgeries. Yet to this day, he stands before thousands of veterans and extends his scarred hand to welcome them home.

From the day Dave Roever said, "Welcome home" to me, I have not been the same. Dave became a friend. Since that day, whenever I meet a Vietnam veteran I always tell them, "Welcome home." May I suggest that you do the same? You will bless those veterans and help to heal the pain and shame most of them carried upon returning to the country they served.

When I became the pastor of North Scottsdale Christian church, one of my first guest speakers was Dave Roever. He continues to encourage people all over the world. Dave takes those who served in the Vietnam War back to Vietnam. He has told me veterans have experienced emotional healing from going back to the place where they served. If you would like to know more about Dave go to his website, The Roever Foundation.

When I think of my friends who served in Vietnam, my first thought is the Vietnam Veterans Memorial in Washington, DC. Today many refer to this as simply, "The Wall."

There were several men from my high school in Phoenix who lost their lives in Vietnam. All of their names are etched on The Wall. There is one name that is extremely important to me. His name was Edward Bohannon. Ed and I went to elementary and high school together. He was the most popular guy at South Mountain High School. I was the most unpopular. Ed was the quarterback and Homecoming King. With all of his success and visibility, he was still very kind to me. We were miles apart on the popularity scale in high school, but Ed would see me and make a point to talk about how long we had gone to school together. He was my friend.

Sharon and I took our children, Ed and Tricia, to Washington, D.C. when they were teenagers. I wanted all of us to be together when I visited the Vietnam Memorial Wall. As my family walked with me trying to find Edward Bohannon's name on the wall, I was wondering if we would ever locate my school friend. A young lady walked up to us with instructions explaining how to find one name among the over 58,000 that were on the wall. Soon, I saw it, there it was. At first it seemed so surreal. Then I had an intense feeling of hurt for Ed Bohannon's family. Our family became silent and could not even talk to each other. Then we all received the comfort of the Holy Spirit. My wife, Sharon, took a piece of tracing paper the young lady had given us and brought forth Edward's name from the wall. As I looked at my son, Ed (named after Ed Bohannon), I was so thankful he would not have to go to war. Then I looked at our daughter, Tricia, and prayed she would not have to go through what my wife experienced. Today my prayer is that the families of those who served in Vietnam will know America will honor and stand with them.

Over the past few years I have developed a few friendships with men who served in Vietnam. Pete was a Marine, Roger served in the Air Force, Dave was a Navy man. These are great men who served their country. All these men have overcome the trials of Vietnam. Each one has been a positive influence in my life and the lives of others.

I would be remiss without mentioning again the name of John Parker, who was my closest friend while we served in Vietnam. The months we spent working together at the 90th were a blessing from the Lord. Since I was not a Christian, I did not know much about the comforting words in the Bible. After coming home and accepting Jesus as my Savior, I discovered these words in Proverbs 18:24 *"A real friend sticks closer than a brother."*(NLT) John was a real friend. I value his friendship to this day. May I suggest if you have a friend from your past, try to find and reach out to them. Both of you will be blessed.

As a Christian, I must never take for granted the friend I have in Jesus Christ. He is, and will always be, your friend. If you have not accepted Him as Lord you can do that today. He will be a friend to you from now throughout eternity.

LIFE APPLICATION

Having friends is a wonderful part of life. Being a friend is even better. With my last name being "Friend," I went through a lot of abuse in school. The kids made fun of my name daily. As an adult, many think they have something clever to say when they say to me I must be a friend to everyone. When you think of it, we should try to be a friend to all those we meet. The Bible tells us, as much as it depends with us we should be at peace with everyone. (See Romans 12:18.) A true friend is a friend forever. Let's all try to build a friendship with someone new this week.

"Focus on your blessings, not your misfortunes."

ROY T. BENNETT, AUTHOR

CHAPTER 14

Blessed in Vietnam

We must tell our children to always look for the good in every situation. That means in every person and every trial. We have all heard the statement, "Every cloud has a silver lining." Well, in Vietnam that was not easy to do; I saw a lot of clouds but they were all lined with the silhouettes of war. It is very difficult to find anything good that happened during the Vietnam War. Allow me to try and point out something positive in an almost impossible, negative, destructive war.

The troops in Vietnam were from every race, ethnicity, financial status, and educational background. With these backgrounds, we learned how to work together. During my year I saw men who started out hating each other become friends. Men who hardly knew one another would be willing to give their lives for someone else.

Don't misunderstand me, I would have preferred to be blessed somewhere other than Vietnam. But, in life we sometimes have to play with the hand that we have been dealt.

There were three events that blessed my life in Vietnam. The first was my assignment to the 90th Replacement Battalion. After a few weeks of being at the 90th I could see how I was blessed by not going into a combat infantry division. To some, it may not have been the best assignment in Vietnam, but it was the one that I got and I had to make the best of it. Throughout our lives we will face both good and bad circumstances. The words of the Apostle Paul found in Philippians 4:11-14 will carry us through all our circumstances. Let me paraphrase what Paul said: He had learned to be content with whatever he had. He learned the secret of living in every situation. That secret was to believe that he could face everything through Christ who gave him strength. That applies to all of us today. (NLT)

My second blessing happened when I requested a leave to go home before my wife gave birth to our first child. My commanding officer said the request had little chance of being approved. However, he would see what he could do. Then he added, "Don't get your hopes up." The number of times we are told that throughout life can be discouraging. I was not a Christian in Vietnam but as a believer in Christ today, my hopes are up all the time. My hope is not in my circumstance but in my Lord.

Sharon and I prayed for God's help in getting my request approved. Without any notice, my commanding officer called me into his office and said that I had been given a 15-day leave. However, if I did not return by the 15th day I would be absent without leave (AWOL). At that time, I would be listed as a deserter. Evidently not all the troops who went on a leave from a combat zone would return. Back in the states, young men were burning their draft cards, leaving the country, and protesting against The Vietnam War and its veterans. My commanding officer made his point very clear to me.

The next day I left for Phoenix, Arizona. Sharon did not know if my leave had been approved, and there was no way that I could contact her. After finding flights on various military aircraft, I wound up in Phoenix at around 2 AM. Since she did not have a telephone, I could not call to let her know that I was in Phoenix. I called my dad and he picked me up at the airport and took me over to her little house. It was about 3am and Dad had to be at work by 7am. Dad was a blessing and was always there for me.

Picture this, Sharon was asleep and not expecting me. I knocked on her door in the middle of the night and within a minute or two she peeked out the window. She looked beautiful in a long nightgown. As she opened the door she said don't look at my stomach. Sharon had sent a few pictures of how she was growing with our baby. But this would be the first time that I would see her in person carrying our child. We hugged and embraced. Sharon was trying to conceal her baby belly. My dad was sitting in the car, so I ran out to him and thanked him for his help. Dad was the best dad a guy could ever be blessed with. He was a friend to everyone. He loved me and all of his children equally. It was one of the best lessons he ever taught me. Thank you, Dad.

Sharon and I spent the night wondering if this was real. How did I get approved? How did I get all those flights without paying for any of them? Today, we give thanks to our God for blessing us in our time of need. *"God is our refuge and strength, always ready to help in times of trouble"* Psalm 46:1 (NLT).

If you are facing a trial, ask God for His help. We were not Christians when I served in Vietnam, but God still came to our rescue. The chances of me receiving a leave while serving in Vietnam were almost impossible. Now we know that we serve a God who makes the impossible reality.

Within about a week, Sharon gave birth to our son Eddie. What a blessing to be able to be there. We were able to take our son home together. He was only four to five days old when I had to find a way to get back to Vietnam and the 90th Replacement Battalion. Sharon and some of my family went out to the National Guard airport in Phoenix. We said our goodbyes and I walked away from Sharon, my brown-eyed girl and our newborn son. That was the most difficult walk I had ever made. Knowing what was in Vietnam made it tougher than when I first went there.

The National Guard flew me to Travis Air Force Base in Northern California. For two days, I tried to get a military flight to Saigon. Not one of the Army, Air Force, or supply planes would allow me to catch a flight. My time of leave had only 24 hours remaining. A military bus took me to the San Francisco airport. Believe it or not, I had to purchase a one-way ticket to Saigon. The cost was around $300. The Army advanced me the funds and said they would take money from my paycheck monthly to pay it back. With only about an hour or two, to spare I reported back to my commanding officer at the 90th. He grinned and said he knew I would not be late. He told me that he had taken a big chance on me and would have been reprimanded by his commanding officer had I not lived up to my commitment.

The third blessing was to go to a USO Bob Hope show on Christmas Day, December 25, 1967. The "USO" stands for "United Service Organization." It is a nonprofit, charitable corporation chartered by Congress. With over 160 centers worldwide, it serves all branches of the United States military. It was founded in 1941.

The show I attended had Bob Hope, Raquel Welch, Miss World, Phil Crosby, and Barbara McNair. It was Christmas morning and I was lonely for my family. One of the men I knew came to me and said that our commanding officer approved the use of a few jeeps to take guys to see Bob Hope. Surprised that Bob Hope was so near and that there was a seat open in one of the jeeps for me, I took off to see the show. Almost everyone knows about the Bob Hope USO shows in Vietnam and around the world during times of war. We had a great time. The laughter was so needed. A buddy of mine had a huge telephoto lens on his camera. The pictures we got made it look like we were on the stage. What a blessing from the Lord on Christmas Day. A great big thank you goes out to the USO for all their work in supporting our veterans.

Regardless of our circumstances the Lord can bless us. The Bible says in everything we must give thanks to the Lord. I am not thankful that I went to Vietnam. However, I am thankful to the Lord for all the blessings he brought to me while I was there.

LIFE APPLICATION

When someone asks us how we are doing, what is our response? Have we ever thought of telling them that we are blessed instead of saying ok? The response I dislike is, "Ok I guess, I am still breathing." We are blessed wherever we go and whatever we do if we realize that all of our blessings come from the Lord. Even during my recent diagnosis of bone marrow cancer I feel blessed. Blessed to see how many are concerned about my condition. Blessed to know that God is in control. Blessed to have great Doctors and medication. In summary, we are all blessed when we look for the blessing.

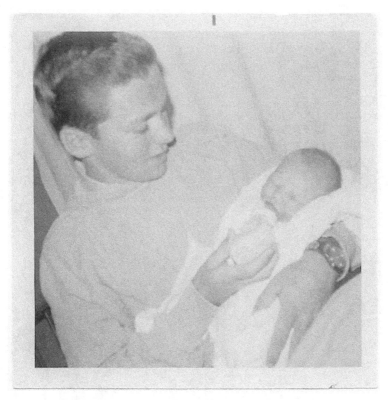

Blessed to be home when Ed was born.

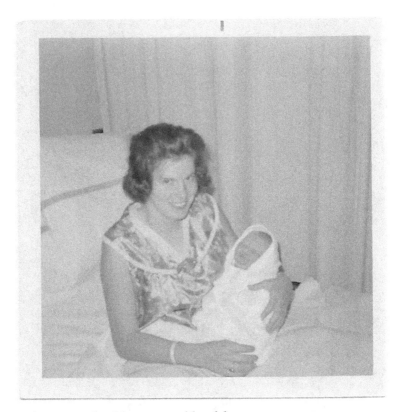

Sharon and Ed happy and healthy.

Blessed to see Bob Hope on Christmas day in Vietnam.

"Never mistake the power of influence."

JIM ROHN, AUTHOR, MOTIVATIONAL SPEAKER

Influence

Vietnam has influenced the lives of millions of Americans. Approximately 2,700,000 men and women served in Vietnam. If my family is typical of the families of just one Vietnam veteran, as many as 50 million family members have been influenced by that war. Husbands, wives, mothers, fathers, children, brothers, sisters and friends have all felt its influence.

When those of us who served in Vietnam came home we were put back into society immediately. There was no follow-up after the veteran went back into civilian life. It seems logical to me that soldiers who have served in a combat area may have been in need of at least a letter or call to see how they were adapting. Had I been contacted, I would have been happy to talk to someone about my feelings. At least I would have felt that someone cared. Our Veterans Administration has dropped the ball in assisting our veterans with their adjustment back into society. The ultimate responsibility rests with our elected representatives.

Allow me to give you an example of my transition back into civilian life. My first thought was don't say anything to anyone. That applied even to my wife. She must have had numerous questions about how I lived, worked, ate, and slept in Vietnam.

My memory recalls talking to Sharon and saying something like this, "Let's not talk about it." Or, "I don't want to bring that into our home." Whatever I said, it was not considerate of the thoughts in her mind. She had to face 365 days of questions and stress while I served. Sharon had to deal with family and friends. For two weeks during the Tet offensive, we could not receive any letters or communication from each other. Sharon, like so many other veteran's wives, was not given assistance in how to deal with their husband returning from a combat zone.

Sharon is the most compassionate person I know. She always puts the feelings of others first. Her strength and understanding of my transition back into our marriage kept us focused on each other and our son. Try to imagine all the wives and families who were going through transition.

The pressure placed on marriages during the Vietnam War was immense. Many of our veterans came home with physical disabilities. Still others had deep emotional scars. The Vietnam soldier was very young. Only about 40% were married.

Because they were older, 65% of World War II veterans were married. Young married couples during Vietnam had the added problem of facing a country divided on its treatment of Vietnam veterans. The influence of Vietnam has destroyed the lives of many of our soldiers who served there.

During my years as a pastor, our church would always do something special on Veterans Day. One such event came from the Vietnam Memorial in Washington, DC. Everyone knows about The Wall with the names of over 58,000 men and women who lost their lives due to action in Vietnam. However, today many Americans are not aware of a bronze sculpture entitled "The Three Soldiers" by Frederick Hart. It stands near The Wall. This sculpture shows three Vietnam veterans dressed in military combat gear. The middle soldier is a Marine. He is wearing an M-1951 body armor vest and armed with a .45-caliber colt pistol. The soldier on the right wears army combat gear with an armored vest. He carries a towel used to absorb his sweat. He has an M-16 rifle. The third soldier is dressed in army fatigues and carries the typical Vietnam gear. To me, these sculptures appear to be a Caucasian, a Hispanic, and an African American. The reason I gave some of the detail is to help you realize how much of an effort it would take if you wanted to build a replica of this memorial.

Well Sharon and I decided to try and put on an illustrated presentation in our church of these three soldiers. We prayed to see how we could bring a representation of the Vietnam sculpture into our church. After approximately two years of praying about this event we decided to try and put it together.

All I could think about was how this could be a way to reach out to the veterans from Vietnam. We did not have a goal to show everyone how creative and talented we were in presenting this living illustration. We just wanted to touch lives.

Sharon and I started going to army surplus stores. We looked online for the belts, boots, jackets, pants, and weapons. The list was extensive, combined with the fact that we were looking for items that were nearly 50 years old. We wanted it to be perfect. This search and rescue mission took between two to three years.

As we went through this process, we met dozens of veterans who worked in these army surplus stores. When we told them that we were putting a living illustration together they were excited. However, when we explained that we would have to spray paint all of these items to make them look like part of a bronze sculpture, they were not sure that they would sell anything to us. When I would told them how this illustration could help so many veterans who were struggling with the influence of their service in Vietnam, we were given the opportunity to purchase whatever we needed.

We were getting close to presenting this on an upcoming Veterans Day weekend. The closer we got, the more concerned I was about how we could get the veterans and their families to come. The church rallied around us and went to the Veterans of Foreign Wars, the VA hospital, and the VA administration office in Phoenix. We invited our mayor, city council, state senators, and representatives. Soon the day came when we would honor all veterans and present the living illustration, "The Three Soldiers."

As the pastor and a Vietnam veteran myself, I felt a great deal of responsibility to present this in a way that would honor our God, country, and veterans. I was nervous and concerned about how this presentation might affect me. The lights went down in the auditorium, the drapes opened, and the living sculpture stood before everyone. At first none of the live actors dressed as Vietnam soldiers moved. They were posing just like that sculpture in Washington, D.C. When they moved into the at ease position you could hear the congregation gasp and then applaud.

As the narrator, I explained the origin of this memorial. When I stopped speaking, each soldier would in turn step down from the small elevated platform we had constructed in the middle of the church stage. They would speak of what may have been on the mind of a soldier serving in Vietnam. Each one spoke of missing family or facing the fear of the unknown. The Holy Spirit had given me the script of what each living sculpture soldier would say. At the end of each soldier's comments they would talk about their comfort in knowing how the Lord would be with them regardless of what they would face.

At the end of this presentation, these soldiers went back to the platform and stood in the same position as the memorial sculpture. The drapes would close and you could hear those in our congregation and veterans sobbing and cheering.

I spoke briefly and asked for those who were not believers in the Lord Jesus Christ to say a prayer of repentance. Dozens in the congregation would give their lives to Christ. Every year, we presented the Vietnam living illustration on Veterans Day weekend. This presentation has been a great influence on the veterans in our community. However, the greatest influence in each of these presentations was the influence of the Holy Spirit bringing those who attended into a personal relationship with Jesus Christ.

Because of the negative influence of the Vietnam War, we hear much today about Post Traumatic Stress Disorder, a.k.a. "PTSD." This affliction may come from various types of trauma. For men, it's usually from physical assault, combat, or a witness to death or injury. Women can experience PTSD from sexual assault and/or child abuse. Approximately 11 to 12% of those who served in Iraq and Afghanistan have experienced PTSD. Up to 30% of veterans from Vietnam have also experienced PTSD at some time in their life.

Upon my return from Vietnam I was so happy to be home that all I thought about was my wife and son. Getting started in a new career and buying a car and home dominated my thoughts. There was no room in my thought life for my experiences in Vietnam.

Then I became a Christian and poured myself into reading God's Word and teaching at our church. Our family attended church every week. We were active in men's and women's groups. Our children grew up in church with all the youth activities. With all of that happening, my thoughts of Vietnam grew less and less.

However, for years I would still dream of being called back to Vietnam. These dreams seemed so real. As time went by, I did not want to watch any of the movies depicting the Vietnam War. Until a few years ago I had avoided movies, books, and discussions about Vietnam. You may ask, then why are you writing this book? That's a real good question. In actuality I never wanted to write about Vietnam.

However, my wife and others have suggested that I give it a try. One day, in the middle of writing a book on generosity my wife said, "You really need to write about your experiences in Vietnam." Something in my heart was touched. Since that day, this book has been my primary focus. My prayer is it will encourage and strengthen those who served in Vietnam and those who were influenced by it.

LIFE APPLICATION

What are we influenced by in life? Everything we read, watch on television, and talk about to others is trying to influence us. Whether we believe it or not, we can be easily influenced. Instead of being influenced, why don't we decide to be an influencer of others. Let's be the one who sees the glass half full and not half empty. Be the positive influence in family conversations. Decide to encourage and build up someone else. Our world needs more of those who try to be a positive influence.

God is shaping us for higher things."

Henry Ward Beecher, American Clergyman

CHAPTER 16

Bone Marrow Cancer: Multiple Myeloma

At this point in my life I could not imagine anything related to Vietnam would ever touch my life again. The church my wife and I founded was doing very well. Our attendance was consistent and so was the income. More importantly, hundreds of individuals had committed their lives to Christ. In the 20 years we pastored, the Lord always provided for our needs. However, something inside of me was saying it's time to step aside and bring a younger pastor in to take over the church. Sharon was the only person with whom I discussed my thoughts. We asked some younger pastors I had known for a number of years to speak on a few Sundays. But they were not the right ones. One day, a friend of ours called me and said he was thinking about moving back to Scottsdale and since I was getting old, maybe I would turn the church over to him. He was a great guy but his approach did not impress me, so I promptly told him no.

About two years went by when I believe the Holy Spirit impressed me to talk to the pastor of my former church. In an unconventional way, the Lord put us together as we ran into each other at a local coffee shop. Within a few months, we merged with his church. The amazing details of the merger will be explained in another book I plan to write.

We were so happy with the success of the merger. Sharon and I thought it was time for us to buy a small home up in the mountains and do some more traveling overseas. We purchased a home in Prescott, Arizona. It needed a major remodel. The remodel seemed like a great idea because now I had time to take on a new project.

Because I am a veteran, I went to the VA hospital in Prescott to have my annual physical check- up. Because I have been challenged with high blood pressure and high cholesterol since I was in my twenties, I needed to check them annually. Even though I have a healthy diet and exercise daily, these areas still need help.

It was about six months after our church merged when I went to the VA Hospital to get my blood tested. The VA doctor reviewed my blood work and said the test results were very good. Normally they would test only my lipid panel. This would include evaluating my cholesterol and triglycerides. The doctor told me for some strange reason my blood tests were done on a much broader area than required. Then he told me he would see me next year and not to worry because everything looked great. I thanked the good doctor and started to leave.

However, before I left something inside of me impressed me to get a copy of the blood tests. It was like a still, quiet voice the Bible talks about. You could call it a whisper which could not be heard audibly. So I asked the doctor if I may have a copy of my blood test results. He kindly gave them to me. Upon being handed the results I realized how extensive these tests were. The next day when I was about to file the blood tests a still, quiet voice made me think about the words, "For some strange reason the tests were done on a much broader area than required." Those words impressed me to ask my family doctor at a clinic in Scottsdale to look over those test results. At first I thought it was not necessary. However, that feeling to get a second opinion on these results became increasingly stronger.

When I contacted my Scottsdale doctor's office, the nurse advised me they usually don't like to look at the results of tests done at a different laboratory than the one they have. However, she would ask the doctor if he would look over my lab tests. After a couple of days the nurse called and said they had seen a couple of things in the test that should be checked further. They drew some more blood and told me to wait for a call. Thinking everything would be just fine I went about my regular activities. After all, I was retired from pastoring the church, now I can relax and have some free time.

We continued with our plans to buy a summer home. It was a Wednesday when we closed on the purchase of our home in Prescott, Arizona. We looked forward to getting into this remodel. The plans we had for this summer home were quite extensive. The day after we closed on the purchase of our Prescott home I received a call from our doctor's office in Scottsdale. The nurse said they wanted to see me the next day.

Sharon and I thought, *What is the urgency?* So we went in and the nurse told us the doctor was out of town and he asked her to give us the results of our blood tests. With a solemn face the nurse advised us there was a strong possibility I had something called Multiple Myeloma, a.k.a. bone marrow cancer. She added this was possibly caused by exposure to Agent Orange in Vietnam.

Sharon and I responded with, "What is multiple myeloma?" We talked with the nurse about possible treatments. As we left the office we were concerned, but not worried.

The doctor referred me to an oncology specialist. Additional tests were needed in order to confirm this preliminary diagnosis. My wife and I were thankful to the Lord because the VA hospital had run such an extensive amount of blood tests.

We also thanked the Lord for the Holy Spirit impressing me to obtain a second opinion. In about a week, we had an appointment with the oncology doctor. He was very kind and after talking to us for about 20 minutes, he told us he was convinced I had multiple myeloma-bone marrow cancer. Then he commented on some very shocking issues.

The good doctor told us he noticed I had served in the Vietnam War. He asked if I had ever had contact with Agent Orange. Quickly I responded with, "Yes. And the area I served in was sprayed with it quite often." The doctor told us not to worry because the treatment of multiple myeloma had come a long way in the past 10 years. He told us, although there is no cure for the disease, he felt I could be cured. We later learned without treatment I could have only six months to live. After leaving the oncologist, Sharon and I went home a little confused.

However, I can honestly say we were not worried. Our trust was in the God we serve.

My first thought was, *Well I can't wait to tell everyone about how the Lord will heal me of this disease.* I told my wife it will be wonderful to be able to stand before the church and tell them about how God has done a miracle in my life.

The thought of dying is not one of my fears. Because I am a Christian, a follower of Jesus Christ, I know I will spend eternity in heaven. As a matter of fact, when the doctor told me of my diagnosis I responded with, "So you are telling me I should be afraid of going to heaven." The second thing I thought about after receiving this diagnosis was, *Why did they spray our military men and women in Vietnam with a chemical capable of killing them?* Fortunately, not everyone who was in Vietnam served in an area sprayed with Agent Orange.

Recently, I have researched the physical destruction Agent Orange has caused in the bodies of those who came in contact with it in Vietnam. During the war our government was aware of the possible negative impact it could have on our troops. Agent Orange has been called one of the risks of war, because it was used to kill off dense foliage where the enemy hid. The danger to our troops would be referred to as "collateral damage."

In 1970, the military decided to discontinue the use of Agent Orange due to the potential harm to our troops. If known, why did they not follow up with those who were exposed to its' toxicity? In my case, the damage Agent Orange did to my body was not discovered until nearly 50 years after my exposure. Had the military taken a simple blood test many years sooner the evidence of Bone Marrow cancer may have been diagnosed earlier. Instead of being proactive in discovering the potential of numerous deadly diseases caused by Agent Orange in the bodies of our troops, our government sits quietly, waiting for the collateral damage to be revealed.

Those of us who spent time in Vietnam had to go through condemnation by war protestors. We went through a time of being ashamed of serving in the war. The transition from serving in a war zone to a factory or office was difficult. Many of the Vietnam Veterans have lifelong physical injuries and mental challenges. Now, decades after leaving Vietnam many face the effects of Agent Orange and PTSD.

Thankfully, I became a Christian about four years after my return from the war. Because of my faith in the Lord Jesus, I have been able to deal with the impact of serving in Vietnam and the diagnosis of bone marrow cancer. Although my assignment was very good compared to what others faced, I believe anyone who serves in a combat zone will have challenges after returning home. This new challenge is just another opportunity to see the hand of my Lord at work in my life.

In 1991, Congress passed the Agent Orange act. This was to study the effects of Agent Orange and set up guidelines on how to help those who were impacted. My prayer is that our government will support all of our veterans. Those who have served from World War II through Afghanistan need the support of the people of the United States of America. Agent Orange is just one more thing our Veterans will continue to need help with for many years.

In my book entitled, *How to Receive Everything in Life from Nothing*, I go into detail of my challenges with Multiple Myeloma. However, here my desire is to show you how the Lord will provide help in our lives when we are going through challenges.

This is a good time to give you an example of how our Lord will take us through the trials we all face. During my initial treatments for Multiple Myeloma, I was put on a large dosage of chemotherapy. One morning my temperature was elevated and I went to the hospital emergency room.

They assigned me to an oncology recovery room. I did not want to spend the night in the hospital. As a matter of fact I could not understand why I could not go home. Yes, I know the Bible tells us in Romans 8:28 *"that in all things God works for the good of those who love Him."* (NIV) However, I was having a struggle understanding how staying in the hospital overnight would work for me. After all, my temperature was good as were all of my tests. Well you probably guessed it, I had to stay. But why?

Soon I understood God's purpose in all of this. The nurse who was assigned to care for me was born in Vietnam. She treated soldiers who had an encounter with Agent Orange. We talked about Vietnam a little and she asked me if I had heard of the city of Bien Hoa. With interest, I told her I had served near the area and our battalion had gone on patrols there. Then she told me her parents had seen the Army patrols near her home. Those patrols had safe-guarded her parents. She thanked me for my service to her parents. Then I thanked her for her service to others and care for me. I told her the Lord knew all about her parents. As He had sent me to protect them, He now has sent her to protect me. I could tell she was deeply touched. This is when I understood why I needed to stay in the hospital for the night. My assignment was to try and talk to her about the Lord.

The next day I was released from the hospital. Since that day, the Lord has kept me free of any infections. In addition, the Lord has kept me from getting sick from vomiting with 28 months of chemotherapy medication.

A nurse advised me it was her opinion after eight months of chemotherapy, prayer, and good doctors, my multiple myeloma was in deep remission. However, the doctors say there is no cure for this disease. Those words will never keep me from believing I am healed. Jesus bore stripes on His back for our healings. We must never doubt those words. I do not know why everyone is not healed from physical illnesses, but Jesus is still our Healer. Besides, as believers in Jesus Christ, our most important healing comes when we join Jesus in Heaven for eternity. We cannot understand all of the issues of children and adults not being healed on earth. But, we will know all about it when we join in Heaven with the children and those who have given their hearts to the Lord Jesus. Until that day, we give the Lord praise for all He has done.

The doctor said there is no cure for this type of cancer. However, every day they get closer to a cure. My medications have been reduced, yet I will remain on a lower dosage for a season. Sharon and I pray every night when I take my chemo pill. We thank the Lord for my complete healing. We know my cure is imminent. In addition, and most important, we know Jesus is our Healer.

Isaiah 53:5-6 gives us comfort when it says,

*"But he (Jesus) was pierced for our rebellion, crushed
for our sins. He was beaten so we could be whole. He
was whipped so we could be healed."* (NLT)
Other translations use the words, *"by his stripes we are healed."*
I pray that Scripture almost every day. We thank the Lord for
His healing touch.

LIFE APPLICATION

Please don't think you must face everything in your life
alone. Our God is omnipresent. He was in the fields of Vietnam and is ready to help all those who call upon Him today
wherever and whoever they are. He is available to be in your life
when you call upon Him.

"Greater love hath no man than this, that a man lay down his life for his friends."

JESUS CHRIST

CHAPTER 17

The Wall

In chapter 13 I wrote about The Vietnam Memorial. a.k.a. "The Wall." Let's look at it from the perspective of being with my family. We waited until our children were teenagers to take them to see The Wall in Washington, D.C. We believed it would make a deeper impact on their lives as teenagers than when they were younger. There is absolutely nothing wrong with taking younger kids to see The Wall; however in our case, I wanted them to try and understand the impact it has made on the lives of millions of Americans, and their Mom and Dad. Because I am a Vietnam Veteran, my wish was to have them connect in some way with the sacrifice our veterans have made so they could live in a free country.

As a history buff, I thought it would be a great family vacation. We went to the capitol building, then the Washington Monument, and the Jefferson and Lincoln memorials. The Smithsonian was a great place to see American history. Our son Ed, and daughter, Tricia, seemed to enjoy seeing a real airplane and space capsule up close. At every stop I would make a comment to our kids about our great leaders. They were probably tired of hearing my history lessons at every junction. However, they never complained to me.

The final stop on our tour that day would be the Vietnam Memorial. It had been dedicated on November 13, 1982. We almost walked by it since it is recessed. Then I saw a black polished granite V- shaped wall. As we walked closer, we could see the names of those who died inscribed on the face of each panel. Over 4 million visit the wall every year. It was built without government funds or additional taxation. Approximately 275,000 Americans, in addition to corporations, foundations, veterans groups, civil organizations, and labor unions, have joined together to give $8.4 million to the project. Over 1,400 designs were submitted for this memorial. A 21-year-old Yale University student, Maya Lin, created the winning design. In 1984 a bronze statue entitled, "The Three Men," representing those who fought in Vietnam, was added to the Memorial. Then in 1993 a bronze statue of three women caring for an injured soldier was placed near the wall.

The wall has the names of over 58,000 Americans who lost their lives due to the war. Names are being added periodically. Every name on the wall has impacted the lives of many Americans. The impact of those who gave their lives have changed millions of American families.

The design of the wall has received worldwide acclamation and condemnation. Some believe the black marble is a sign of disgrace. Others have said the wall cannot be seen until you almost walk into it. Still others feel the wall shows Vietnam as an embarrassment that needed to be hidden. However, millions love the design. Everyone I have met who has seen the wall has been touched by it emotionally. Personally, the Vietnam Memorial wall has shown me America's love for the veterans who have served in Vietnam. My family thought it was amazing.

Recently, Sharon and I have seen a mobile version of the wall. Although significantly smaller, it is just as powerful as the one in Washington, D.C. As a Vietnam veteran, the wall is the most emotional memorial I have ever seen. My wife and I have been blessed to see memorials and monuments in many countries. To us, none of them better represent the sacrifice of those who died fighting a war dividing our country. The wars of World War I, World War II, and Korea were supported by the majority of Americans. Those who have served in the middle east and around the world, now receive respect from their country. Sadly it has taken decades for the Vietnam Veterans to be able to feel honored by America.

One of the reasons the wall was built was to help those who have struggled with Post Traumatic Stress Disorder due to their service in Vietnam. I believe it has helped greatly.

Every young person in our country should visit the war memorials in our nation's capital. There are 15 military monuments, museums and memorials in Washington, D.C.

Following is a list of them:

1) US Marine Corps war Memorial Iwo Jima.

2) Women in military service for America Memorial.

3) United States Air Force Memorial.

4) Vietnam Veterans memorial.

5) Vietnam Women's Memorial.

6) Korean War Veterans memorial.

7) District of Columbia World War II Memorial.

8) Navy- merchant Marine Memorial.

9) World War II Memorial.

10) National Museum of American Jewish military history

11) African American Civil War Museum.

12) Soldiers home.

13) United States Navy Memorial.

14) National Guard Memorial Museum.

15) American veterans disabled for life Memorial.

All of these memorials and museums represent those who served and/or gave their life for their country. All of these brave men and women must be honored. The soldiers of past wars and the modern-day wars of Iraq, Afghanistan, and the Middle East must be given praise for their service.

As Christians, the greatest memorial we have is the cross of Jesus Christ. The Cross represents Christs' death. When the Cross is shown without the body of Jesus Christ, it depicts his resurrection. As I have mentioned in a prior chapter, John 15:13 *"There is no greater love than to lay down one's life for one's best friend."* (NLT) This represents God's love for mankind.

As we all know, the names of the veterans on the Vietnam Memorial wall represent those who gave their life for others.

There are many interesting statistics and stories from the Vietnam Memorial Wall.

There are over 58,000 names listed on The Vietnam Memorial Wall.

The first casualty was Richard Fitzgibbon of North Weymouth, Mass. He was listed by the U.S. Department of Defense as having been killed on June 8, 1956. His name is listed on the wall with his son, Marine Corps Lance Cpl. Richard B. Fitzgib-bon III, who was killed on September 7, 1965.

There are three sets of fathers and sons on the wall.

Approximately 40,000 on the wall were 22 or younger.

8,283 were only 19 years old.

12 soldiers on the wall were 17 years old.

5 soldiers on the wall were 16 years old.

One soldier was 15 years old.

Nearly 1,000 soldiers were killed their first day in Vietnam.

1,448 soldiers were killed on their last day in Vietnam.

31 sets of brothers are on the wall.

54 soldiers attended Thomas Edison High School in Philadelphia.

8 women nurses are on the wall.

244 soldiers were awarded the Medal of Honor during the Vietnam War; 153 are on the wall.

The Marines of Morenci, Arizona had 9 of graduates from Morenci High School enlist in the Marine Corp. Their service began on Independence Day, 1966. Only 3 returned home.

The most casualties for a single day was on January 31, 1968 –245 deaths. The day after The Tet offensive began.

Most deaths for a single month in May 1968 – 2,415 died.

Edward Bohannon, my friend. After attending 12 years of elementary and high school together, he gave his life in Vietnam.

Our son Edward is honored with the name of my friend.

Most Americans who read these statistics will see only numbers of fatalities. To those of us who survived the war, and to the families, classmates, and friends of those who did not, we see the faces, we feel the pain these numbers represent.

As a follower of Jesus Christ I am thankful for His hand of protection over me in Vietnam. Although I did not confess Him as my Lord and Savior, He gave His life so I would have eternal life with Him.

LIFE APPLICATION

Our country has been blessed with men and women who have put their lives on the line to defend this nation and people around the world. We must never stop giving honor to those who serve and have served in our armed forces.

"Mankind must put an end to war before war puts an end to mankind."

PRESIDENT JOHN F. KENNEDY

After the War

Although most of the Vietnam Veterans are in their 60s and 70s they have a lot of good years ahead of them. At the age of 71, I have never felt more proud of my Vietnam service. After 50 years or so of trying to forget everything, it's amazing how much comes back to my mind.

Today it is easy to talk with other veterans. However, I still do not want to watch some of the Hollywood versions of Vietnam. When I meet other veterans, it seems most of us have a similar experience with how Vietnam has affected us. Personally, I rarely spoke about my time there unless someone brought up the topic. However, as I entered my mid 60s it seemed to be okay to discuss my service with other veterans. I must admit I can become a little emotional at times with certain aspects of my Vietnam experiences.

Some have told me the reason for this feeling coincides with this stage of my life. Most 65 to 70 year-olds feel free to discuss almost anything. Think about it for a moment. We have completed our career cycle. Our children are grown and have families of their own. Now, we have a little extra time to think each day. Could it be there are tens of thousands of senior citizens mentally reliving some of their past Vietnam experiences?

This could lead to an increase in senior citizens experiencing Post Traumatic Stress Disorder late in life. To be very honest, a little bit of PTSD pops up in my life occasionally. However, once again, as a believer in the Lord Jesus Christ I can receive strength from my faith in Him.

My favorite Scripture for dealing with the pressures of life comes in the Apostle Paul's words to the church in Philippi. It's found in Philippians 4:6-8,

> *"Don't worry about anything; instead, pray about everything. Tell God what you need, and thank Him for all he has done. Then you will experience God's peace, which exceeds anything we can understand. His peace will guard your hearts and minds as you live in Christ Jesus. And now, dear brothers and sisters, one final thing. Fix your thoughts on what is true, and honorable, and right, and pure, and lovely, and admirable. Think about things that are excellent and worthy of praise."*(NLT)

If we could all just get into our hearts and minds to do just the first four words of verse six. "Don't worry about anything." Think about it, what an accomplishment it would be for us. It would also be a blessing to those who we participate with in life.

It has been over 50 years since I served in Vietnam. Since then, I have experienced many good, and some bad, things in my life. In the past years of your life you can probably say the same thing. Let me suggest you take a moment and write down all the good events in your life. By doing this it may temporarily remove the thoughts of some of your bad experiences.

In America today, those who served in Vietnam have a place of honor and respect in our country. They are no longer insulted and made to feel ashamed of their service. It seems I see Vietnam bumper stickers, caps, T-shirts everywhere I go. But I also see those who are suffering physically and mentally with what they experienced many decades ago. We must do our best to help those veterans in need.

When I visit the VA hospital in Prescott, Arizona, I am fortunate to see doctors, nurses, pharmacists, technicians, and others who serve all of our veterans. Those who work in the Prescott VA hospital are kind and caring. My personal experience in Prescott has been excellent. Those who have helped me have been friendly and almost always thank me for my service. Well, I want to thank all of those in Prescott for their service to our Veterans and to our country.

As we know, the Veterans Administration in America has seen a significant amount of criticism over the past decade. In my humble opinion, a large portion of it is deserved. However, the majority of those who work for the VA are doing their best to help others. As in most organizations, there are good and poor employees.

We must hold our government accountable for the care of our veterans. As voters we need to demand that our representatives in Congress improve the operation of the Veterans Administration. Just as important, we must pray for veterans. They need our help and encouragement. These men and women served and are serving our country without concern for their own well-being.

As you can tell, Vietnam has played a significant role in my life. In addition, it has influenced the lives of over 2,700,000 men and women since the early 1960s who served there. As a 19-year-old man I could have never anticipated how the next two years would impact my life. As teenagers we all think we will live forever and we can try anything, eat anything, and live anyway we desire. As we grow older, we can look back at how the influences in our life have impacted us and others. May those of us who have some years of experience use those experiences to help someone else. May America benefit from past experiences and help those who may be challenged by their past.

When the impact of something like war touches the lives of so many, something must change. That change will influence everything we will do today and in the future.

These are the reasons why I entitled my book *Vietnam: Before, During, and After, A Young Man's Journey*. The influence of Vietnam made me look at life and death differently. As a teenager I wanted to live life to its fullest. When I saw death in Vietnam, especially the deaths of young men with whom I went to school, it made me realize the fragility of life.

King David wrote in Psalm 39:4 *"Lord, remind me how brief my time on earth will be. Remind me that my days are numbered — how fleeting my life is."* (NLT) When I realized how quickly we can pass from life into eternity, I decided to find out what eternity had in store for me. Most of us live our lives focused entirely on today. The temporal should never be our only thought. As a Christian, I have discovered God looks at eternity in everything he advises us to do in this life. His desire is for us to live a good life. He wants to bless us in everything we do. However, He wants us to prepare for eternity.

All of His plans for our lives on earth are devoted to how we will spend eternity with Him. Believe it or not, Vietnam has benefited me for eternity. Even Multiple Myeloma has helped me to help others who are facing a terminal illness.

First, I can show them how to make the most of living. They can give and receive forgiveness. They can love others like they never imagined possible.

Secondly, they can prepare for eternity with Christ and lead as many as possible to become His followers.

How about you? Do you know where you will spend eternity? The answer to my question is found in one of the most quoted scriptures in the Word of God.

> *"For this is how God loved the world: He gave his*
> *one and only Son, so that everyone who believes in*
> *Him will not perish but have eternal life."*
> John 3:16 (NLT)

If you have not done so before, ask the Lord to forgive you of your sins. Believe Jesus is the son of God. Accept Him as your Lord and Savior. Promise to serve Him all the days of your life.

Now, find a good Bible-believing church. Ask the pastor if he believes in John 3:16 and if he understands the prayer you just prayed to the Lord. This does not make you perfect. However it starts a relationship between you and the only true and perfect One, the Lord Jesus Christ. May the Lord bless you and keep you. May He shine His blessings upon you, and give you peace.

LIFE APPLICATION

To those who served in Vietnam and other wars, may you receive help from reading these experiences. The Lord had His hand on me even though I had not given my life to Him.

Welcome home and thank you for your service.

To those who had loved ones in Vietnam, I pray you will have a better understanding of what they went through.

Never miss the opportunity to thank our veterans for their service.

Back to our home state. We bought our 1968 Camaro in California. Life was good again. My dream wife, car, and son..

"There is only one way to avoid criticism do nothing, say nothing, and be nothing."

ARISTOTLE

CHAPTER 19

Looking Back: My Opinion

So many times we have heard it said to never look back. Even the Bible warns us of the dangers of looking back. Remember the story of Lot's wife looking back at the cities of Sodom and Gomorrah? When she looked back, she turned into a pillar of salt. (See Genesis 19.) Jesus warns us not to look back.

Is it ever acceptable to look back? Well, I think that it is. Before you think I am taking issue with what the Bible teaches, please hear me out.

In all of these warnings about looking back, we discover they were referring to looking back in order to go back and live that life again. In calling this chapter "Looking Back," I am referring to using what we have learned in the past to help us live a better life in the future. When looking back to Vietnam we see hundreds of questions tied to the war. Following is a list of what I call the "Why's of Vietnam." As a pastor, I never cared for the word "why." It sounded so much like whining. However, in looking back to my service in Vietnam, I must admit I had a lot of why's. Before, during, and after my tour of duty I thought a lot about why we ever went to Vietnam. To each question I try to give my opinion, for whatever it's worth.

One of my commanding officers told me to never ask why. He always told us to do it or die. That advice may have been helpful to run an army, but in life it's almost never true.

Question: Why do men volunteer to go to war?
Response: It may be love of country or compassion for those being abused. Family or peer pressure may sometimes be the reason.
Question: Why did I think we were there to fight communism?
Response: My president said that was the reason and I actually believed him. Today I don't trust most politicians.

Question: Why did I not want to talk to anyone about Vietnam after I returned?
Response: I was ashamed of my service in Vietnam. I accepted the words of those who hated Vietnam Veterans.

Question: Why did we care if communism took this tiny country?
Response: Communism has failed everywhere it has been attempted. It robs people of living free.

Question: Why did we have all the division back home?
Response: Most felt our troops were dying for no reason. Later we discovered it was true.

Question: Why did President Johnson put 500,000 troops in danger?

Response: To prove he was a tough Texan.

Question: Why did I volunteer for the draft?

Response: The recruiter promised me a good assignment. In addition, it was only a two-year commitment.

Question: Why didn't I just enlist in the Army?

Response: It was a four-year commitment.

Question: Why did they need a personnel specialist in a war zone?

Response: Someone had to do it. Eighty percent of those in Vietnam were support groups for the combat troops.

Question: Why did some of our men think of the enemy as not being human?

Response: There were those who did not believe God created everyone equal. Others saw the Vietcong's inhumanity to man and wanted them to experience it.

Question: Why has the Veterans administration been so ineffective?

Response: Another example of governmental malfunction. Lack of Congressional and community support.

Question: Why did it take 30 to 40 years after the war before Vietnam Veterans would receive respect from its country?
Response: Time heals many wounds.

Question: Why did the Marines or Army take over a hill and leave it only a few days later?
Response: Our conventional war tactics did not work in Vietnam.

Question: Why are there so many homeless veterans in the U.S.?
Response: Due to a lack of government and public interest.

Question: Why was it called an unpopular war?
Response: Over half of our country opposed it because Congress and our President lied to them.

Question: Why did they protest the veterans when they came home, when they were protesting for veterans to come home?
Response: Many times protesters overlook the reason for their protest. Radical protesters were driven by radical ideas.

Question: Why did 30,000 young American men run to Canada to dodge the draft?
Response: Some due to fear of going to war, others did not understand the options available to them.

Question: Why did 30,000 young Canadian men volunteer to help America in Vietnam?

Response: They thought they were fighting against communism, or wanted to back American soldiers.

Question: Why did the military use Agent Orange in Vietnam when so many knew it was toxic and could cause cancer?

Response: Just another government error. Some considered any danger to our soldiers would be collateral damage.

Question: Why didn't I protest the war instead of going there?

Response: My father and uncle were in World War II. My brother, Jim, and brother-in-law, Rich, served in the Air Force. When our government called on me to serve, I said yes, no questions asked.

Question: Why did some burn their draft cards?

Response: It was an outward expression of an inward desire. It proved nothing to the draft board. Kind of like a woman who burned her bra, there was no way to support it.

Question: Why do 22 Vietnam Veterans commit suicide every day?

Response: They have no purpose or hope. Only our Lord Jesus can give hope. Only God can give us purpose.

Question: Why did General Westmoreland request another 200,000 troops?

Response: In war most generals feel we cannot lose if we have overwhelming strength on the ground. In the future that is not how we will fight our wars.

Hopefully the why's listed above have helped some better understand Vietnam. Before you disagree with my responses, realize many of these whys' could become a book in itself. Today, I don't have any why's about my service in Vietnam. They have been replaced with my trust in my Lord and Savior Jesus Christ. My prayer is you will turn the why's in your life into faith in our Lord. Remember Proverbs 3:6,

"Trust in the Lord with all your heart: do not depend on your own understanding. Seek His will in all you do, and He will show you which path to take."(NLT)

ABOUT THE AUTHOR

David Friend began his education at Phoenix College but was interrupted by serving in the military in Vietnam. Upon completing his service and returning to the United States, he graduated from Phoenix College. He studied finance and lending at Western Bancor. He later worked as a part-time instructor in banking at seven community colleges in Arizona.

While working at First National Bank and First Interstate Bank from 1969 to 1984, he served as Operations Officer and Branch Manager, Commercial Lender, Vice-President and Regional Manager, and State Retail Sales Manager.

David was a Vice President and in partnership with a real estate development company for three years. He then owned and operated his own development firm, Dave Friend Homes, from 1987 to 1997.

In 1997, he went into full-time ministry at Phoenix First Assembly. He was ordained in 1998 and started a new church, called North Scottsdale Christian. During David's time as Senior Pastor, the Lord blessed the church with over 1,000 members. In 2015, North Scottsdale Christian merged with Phoenix First Assembly, to create Dream City Church.

Currently, David serves as a board member with Dream City Church. He is mentoring businessmen and speaks on finance and prayer.

David has served as a board member for Teen Challenge, Grand Canyon University Foundation, Tucson Salvation Army, and several local churches.

He resides in Scottsdale, Arizona with his wife, Sharon. Together, they have two married children and six grandchildren.

CPSIA information can be obtained
at www.ICGtesting.com
Printed in the USA
BVHW04s0613231018
530984BV00006B/24/P

9 781640 881358